MAMA
a poet's heart in a Kentucky girl

Our circle will never be broken:
In memory of Paddy Baker and Edwin Whitehead

Ron and Greta Whitehead have created a soulful, folksy and important masterpiece. The book brings us closer to Kentucky, closer to family, closer to humanity.—Frank Messina, author, actor, and the New York Mets Poet Laureate

A lovely homage not only to Ron Whitehead's beloved mother Greta Render Whitehead but to all their kin, the poems and stories in MAMA will make you laugh and weep and wonder. These are the tales of ordinary people, told by a mother and son who see the world in a most extraordinary way.—Bobbi Buchanan, poet, professor, publisher of NEW SOUTHERNER

Ron Whitehead continues his legacy. With humor, tears, and an abundance of love, he has written a lasting tribute to a remarkable woman, MAMA.—Nancy Bruner Wilson, poet, author

MAMA is a beautiful and entertaining collaboration between Mother and Son. It is not only their story but a true life story of a place and time in Kentucky.—Michael Dean Odin Pollock, legendary Iceland musician

OTHER BOOKS BY RON WHITEHEAD

Beaver Dam Rocking Chair Marathon
Blood Filled Vessels Racing to the Heart
Ghost Lover, Trance Mission
I Refuse I Will Not Bow Down I Will Never Give Up
I Will Not Bow Down
Kokopelli
Mama: a poet's heart in a Kentucky girl, photo edition
Searching for Jack Kerouac
The Declaration of Independence This Time: Selected Poems
The Storm Generation
The Storm Generation Manifesto & On Parting
The Third Testament: Three Gospels of Peace
The Wanderer
We See the Sound of Setting Sun
Western Kentucky: Lost & Forgotten, Found & Remembered

AUDIO RECORDINGS

Exterminate Noise
From Iceland to Kentucky & Beyond
I Refuse
I Will Not Bow Down
Kentucky Blues
Kentucky Roots
Kentucky: poems, stories, songs
Pack My Soul in Dry Ice
Ron Whitehead and Southside's Southside Lounge
Ron Whitehead and Southside's We Are the Storm double-CD
Searching for Jack Kerouac
Swan Boats @ Four
Tapping My Own Phone
The Bonemen
The Shape of Water
The Storm Generation Manifesto & On Parting
The Viking Hillbilly Apocalypse Revue
Trance Mission
Walking Home

MAMA
a poet's heart in a Kentucky girl

Ron Whitehead
and Greta Render Whitehead

TRANCEMISSION PRESS
Historic Clarksville | Indiana

The authors wish to thank the many friends and family members who contributed photographs for this book and the limited edition hardbound book. Thank you Angela Wass for transcribing the interviews. Thank you Nancy Bruner Wilson for proof reading. And a special thank you to Jinn Bug for her beautiful production work and for her poem "Iconoclast", which appears at the close of this book.

Editors: Ron Whitehead and Jinn Bug
Layout, graphic design and production by Jinn Bug

Copyright © 2015 by **Ron Whitehead and Greta Render Whitehead**

All rights reserved. No part of this publication may be reproduced, distributed or transmitted in any form or by any means, without prior written permission.

**Trancemission Press
301 S Clark Blvd
Clarksville IN 47129
www.trancemission.xyz**

MAMA: a poet's heart in a Kentucky Girl, Ron Whitehead and Greta Render Whitehead. – 1st ed.
ISBN-13: 978-0692537145/ISBN-10: 0692537147

1

My first real home was a small mining house that my Dad and uncle moved from Matanzas to Walton's Creek.

They placed the house close to The Montgomery Brothers' family home. They moved the house in the afternoon and we stayed in it that night. The next morning The Montgomery Brothers went to get their mail and they were shocked to see a house up the lane with people in it.

When it came to fixing up a place to live my Mom and Dad were magic. In one day Daddy added a kitchen to the back and Mama had the whole house decorated. We moved from there to Fordsville, Bowling Green, Vine Grove, Louisville, Elizabeth, Indiana and back to Centertown.

My Dad barbered in all these places. At Vine Grove we lived in our car and tent as Daddy helped build the Muldraugh Hill as grader man and more. He went on to work at Jeffersonville ship yard building PT boats during WWII. That's when we lived in Elizabeth, Indiana. We had a large garden. Mama and I sold produce Saturday mornings at the New Albany farmer's market.

My parents got homesick so we moved back to Centertown and opened The Blue Bus Café.

2

Daddy discovered an abandoned Greyhound Silverside bus in the woods below Centertown. He moved it to town and made it into The Blue Bus Café.

That was during WWII. Everything was rationed but Mama used their war stamps, and her Mom's too, to buy sugar for lemonade as well as her delicious grilled cheese sandwiches and hamburgers.

The Blue Bus Café was a great place to eat while sitting in a booth and listening to the juke box music. You could also sit by the fireplace and visit. My Dad was always busy in his Barber Shop and couldn't drive my Mom to places she needed to go so he told me I would have to drive her.

It was 1945 and I was 13 when he took me to the Court House and asked Judge Blankenship if he could give me my driver's license. I took no test whatsoever. He simply gave me my license. I could already drive well from driving my Dad's Model T.

When I married my parents moved back to Louisville for my Dad to work on building the Watterson Expressway doing grader work. That's where the grader turned over on him. He lived a week. That was 1959.

3

When Daddy died my Mom was in her 40s. She had four boys to raise, alone. She and my sisters went to Beauty School and got their licenses. Mama opened a shop in her basement.

When my youngest brother was a teenager she moved back to Centertown and built her a cute little house. She got to join the Walton's Creek Homemakers again. She was a Charter Member. Jo and I were also Charter Members because we went to meetings way back when we were little girls.

But I learned to cook and wash laundry as I waited on my Mom while she was having babies. I'm the oldest of 13. I washed diapers on a washboard and hung them on clothes lines to dry.

But I had fun as a kid. When we moved to Centertown we had free range of the town. We had many friends to play games with. We played Hopscotch, Hide and Seek, Kick the Can, and games we made up. We had a nice Skating Rink. My Dad and I could skate really well.

4

It's hard to realize I'm over 80. I don't feel like it. Maybe because I don't dress old. I said years ago that I will NOT wear old ladies shoes or clothes.

The stylists say if you want to look younger wear your collar turned up. Not down like old women. One Sunday at church I had my collar up and an older lady turned it down thinking I had forgot. I said thanks but I wear it up to look younger.

I get noticed from guys my sons' age and I like it. They like me because I'm up beat. I say thanks and then think of my 90 year old guys I have breakfast with. I miss my sweet Ed especially when I watch a love story movie or hear certain songs. But I get a thrill when I get together with my family to hear them sing and tell stories of their trips. I have a singing family along with writers and poets. We have performed many concerts to benefit certain people including the sick. I am blessed.

Greta Render Whitehead

Throughout this book, "GRW" indicates writing by Greta Render Whitehead, while 'RW" indicates selections by Ron Whitehead.

Contents

Mama 1
Mama a poet's heart in a kentucky girl 2
a child is born 4
I've Always Loved Being the Oldest of 13 5
In 1937 We Took a Boat to Bowling Green 7
When We Lived in Our Car 9
When We Lived in Our Chicken House 12
I Dream of Iduma Best in Elizabeth Indiana 15
a league of her own 17
oh what a wonderful honeymoon 19
ronnie paige 21
Your Dad's Badge 23
3 dead peckers 24
The Entertainer 25
No Greater Love 26
To Our Six Babies 28
Bloomer Joined the Circus 29
Precious Memories 30
our first our last our next kiss 32
the night watch 34
quilting in deep snow 38
the year granddaddy died 41
a master of checkers 42

boys it's time to hoe	44
wrestling hercules	46
the boxer	49
if it be your will dear god please help me grow	52
Moxley and Eirene Moonshine King Burgoo Queen	54
mama's little helper	59
old blue	62
i hate suckering tobacco	64
song of the auctioneer	68
in kentucky	72
stevie fell out	74
arriving	76
the dance	79
a week before Christmas	81
Mama and Daddy Taught Me	82
The Sound of Snowflakes on Christmas Eve	83
the old singing barn	86
Thanksgiving in Kentucky	91
loneliness	95
square bales ain't square and neither am i	97
mourning my father	99
at the walton's creek graveyard	100
I Loved the Stage	101
HellFire and Brimstone Electric Chair Evangelist	102
Turnip and Mink Christmas	103
Dear President Reagan	104
We Were All Thrifty in Those Days	106
It Surely Says Heaven	108

The Old Home Place	110
Come Home to Bluegrass	112
Look Up and Look Beyond	114
THE INTERVIEWS: Ron Interviews Mama	115
Acknowledgements	207
About the Authors	208
Afterword	211

Mama

Mama killed chickens. She popped their heads off. Put her foot on the little hen's head, grabbed its legs and jerked hard. The head just laid there on the grass while the little chicken body went flopping all over the yard. Us kids ran like crazy dodging chicken blood. I liked it better when Mama took the .22 rifle to the barn and would shoot a little hen off the high rafter up near the top of the barn where the chickens all roosted. Mama was a good shot.

One Christmas Eve there was a terrible storm. Daddy was off at the mines. Mama said "come on" and all us kids piled into the back of the old pickup truck. Mama had the shotgun. We drove slow through the storm with Mama looking all round then she pulled over and said "come on." We followed. We walked a ways until we came up on a tree, a cedar tree, and Mama said "get behind me." We did and she took aim and shot the tree in the trunk with both barrels. Blew it clean in two. Mama said "y'all get the Christmas tree and come on."

Us kids let out a yell! We were so happy cause Christmas had finally come.

RW

Mama
a poet's heart in a kentucky girl

when i was a boy time and again
always in a hurry i ran in through the back screen door

of our old farmhouse looking for a ball or glove
and out of the corner of my eye i saw

mama writing in her spiral notebook
mama's work was never done

she worked night and day
but she always found time to write a few words

then she'd hide her notebook away
to the kitchen the garden the barn the field

to work she forever went
when i woke up in the mornings

when i went to bed at night
mama was working working working

but i never once in all my life
heard mama complain

last night late as i was reading
mama's handwritten notes i found

one written on the back of a torn envelope
the note was written to daddy it said

when all the children leave home
i'm going to become a writer

things have changed so much for women
in the 82 years mama has shared with us here on earth

but women still aren't fully equal to men
they're still paid less for doing the same jobs

and in some countries they're still slaves
but it sure makes me happy

that mama is so excited to be
writing this book with me

mama's always been a writer
and god willing in 2015

greta render whitehead will be
a published author with a book in her name

a poet's heart in a kentucky girl
mama

RW

a child is born

on an old winding tree lined dirt kentucky backroad
on may 23rd in the year of our lord 1932
in her igleheart grandparents' handmade home
on a feather bed
a child is born

greta render
oldest of 13

greta render whitehead
mother of 6
grandmother of 18
greatgrandmother of 26
a child is born

                              RW

I've Always Loved Being the Oldest of 13

Mama loved Daddy so much she'd go
to bed with him anytime he wanted to

Well the proof is in the pudding you see
On May 23, 1932 I was born on a feather bed

At our little home near Matanzas
Outside Centertown not far from the Green River

Louverine Igleheart and Raymond Thomas Render
Were so in love anywhere Daddy went Mama would go

It wasn't long after I was born that
I had 12 sisters and brothers

To some of them I became a 2nd mother
Jo Carolyn was born in 1933

Adeline in 1935 Kendall Ray in 1937
Linda Ann in 1939 Rebecca Sharon in 1942

Eddie Bennett in 1944 Donna Jill in 1945
Danny Boy in 1947 Steven Lee in 1949

Suzanne in 1950 Timothy Allen in 1951
And lucky 13 Jody Todd in 1958

Well Eddie and Suzanne and Linda are gone
And we'll join them eventually but

I hope to see all those still here with their families
At the Annual Render Reunion

In Elizabethtown Kentucky
I've always loved being the oldest of 13

GRW

In 1937 We Took a Boat to Bowling Green

a man didn't put his cigarette butt out good
so when he tossed it into a pile of dirty rags

daddy's barber shop on main street in
fordsville burned down my sister jo carolyn

and i stayed at pappy render's near matanzas
while mama and daddy got us a room over

a restaurant on western kentucky university's
campus in bowling green well it was

western kentucky state teachers college back then
daddy's new barber shop was next door

to the restaurant and our new home
i was 5 years old in 1937

the year of the great flood
somehow daddy made it to pappy's near

matanzas and took jo and me to
our new home in bowling green

we had to go most of the way in a boat
western's campus was so pretty the big hill

and tree lined sidewalks i'll never forget
the easter parade the beautiful ladies

with colorful hats the marching bands
and the giant bunny rabbits

i made friends with the little boy across the hall
i loved his bright black rubber boots so much

he let me try them on but they got stuck
and it took my aunt ruthie who had come

to visit she was 16 plus mama and
the little boy's mother from across the hall

to pull those bright black rubber boots off me
no matter where we lived daddy worked hard

he was the best barber he told stories
while he cut hair everyone loved him

including me i loved daddy so much
daddy had gypsy blood all us renders do

he always wanted to travel
he always wanted to stay home

in 1937 we took a boat to bowling green
                                        GRW

When We Lived in Our Car

mama and daddy loved each other so much
that wherever daddy's work took him we all

packed up and went we really were gypsies
and no matter where we lived we had fun

it was 1943 during world war 2
i was 11 when we lived in our car

daddy got a job as grader operator
building muldraugh hill so we moved to

vine grove daddy barbered at night
and worked on dixie highway during

the day daddy found us a place in
downtown vine grove it was a small

and friendly town i'm the oldest of 13 so
when i was 11 there was jo carolyn and

adeline and kendall and linda and becky

jo and i made our bed in the trunk
of course we kept the top open

daddy could build anything so he
threw a tarp over the back of the car

so adeline and linda had a tarp tent
while kendall slept in the front seat

of the car and becky in the back seat
then mama and daddy had their own

separate tent not far from us mama
cooked on our campfire she

believed that cleanliness was next
to godliness so everything was always

spic and span plus she always made
all our clothes by hand we had such a

grand grand time we made friends with
everyone we met in vine grove we've

always been a friendly family we love
people and we're good neighbors we

always clean up after ourselves and
we always offer others a helping hand

at night after supper which some folks
call dinner we sat around our campfire

and told stories and sang songs daddy was
a master storyteller and singer he had

such a beautiful tenor voice and he could
play any instrument he picked up

mama and daddy were such good
people they loved life and so do i

i'm thankful for every minute of it
no matter where we lived it was fun including

when we lived in our car

GRW

When We Lived in Our Chicken House

when daddy finished his grader operator
work on muldraugh hill dixie highway

we moved from vine grove and living
in our car to the algonquin park area

in louisville it was so much fun
when we lived in our chicken house

uncle paul mabrey had sold his chickens
and cleaned everything up and put in

a little wood stove that mama cooked on
plus it kept us warm in cold weather

mama and daddy could do anything
mama painted flowers on the windows

with a bon ami soap bar and she painted
big yellow sunflowers on the linoleum floor

our chicken house was one big room
where we all lived jo carolyn and i walked

through algonquin park to school i loved
school mama handmade our clothes

we were always fashionable it was during
world war 2 so there were blackouts

we peeked out the windows and watched
the big lights crisscrossing the sky at night

we sang when the lights come on again
all over the world daddy had a job at

jeffboat building ship-tanks and
submarine chasers plus he barbered

during his lunch breaks 2 years ago
the doctor found a spot on my lungs

he said i had probably been around
chickens when i was young and

of course i was always around chickens
ronnie paige do you remember when

we ordered little baby chickens and
they came in the mail you loved them

you know i don't pay too much attention
to doctors i learned a long time ago that

a good attitude is
the best medicine of all

it was so much fun
when we lived in our chicken house

GRW

I Dream of Iduma Best in Elizabeth Indiana

Mama yelled Slow Down Raymond
Daddy loved to drive fast over the roller coaster

Hills of southern Indiana outside Elizabeth
Where we moved after living in our chicken house

In 1944 World War II was still going on and
Daddy was still working at Jeffboat building

Ship-tanks and submarine chasers and
He found us the sweetest little home

In Elizabeth Indiana we had a huge garden
I was only 12 years old but on Saturdays

I drove Mama to the New Albany Farmer's Market
Where we sold vegetables from our garden

At night and on weekends Daddy cut hair
In a brand new barber shop in Elizabeth

We had so many friends in Elizabeth
My best friend was Iduma Best

That really was her name we loved
The Best family Iduma's sister Bobby

Was deaf but she was smart and pretty
She traveled with Daddy and others back

And forth to Jeffboat in Jeffersonville she
Worked there too Iduma and I caught

Big crawdads in the branch and cooked
Them over an open fire they were delicious

My sister Jo Carolyn and I picked raspberries
At the raspberry farm

I remember the long winding Ohio River hill
I dream of Iduma Best in Elizabeth, Indiana

GRW

a league of her own

mama never smoked or chewed tobacco but
she could sure play softball

in 1943 the first professional female
baseball league became a big hit

12 years later i was playing in dirt
on the centertown ball park playground

watching mama windmill windup then let
loose firing fast pitch softball striking

out batter after batter 3 up 3 down then
when her turn came to bat she stepped up

to the plate and drove line drive after line
drive down the right field then left field lines

and straight up the middle whether
pitching or hitting mama had perfect aim she

could place the ball wherever she wanted
and on defense nobody could hit the ball

by her she had a good glove and on offense
she was greased lightning running bases

she was a complete team player
a few years back she was an extra

for the film a league of their own she
met geena davis and madonna at

bosse field in evansville mama and i
love that film we love sports and we

believe in equal rights for women i've never
met anyone quite like mama she's in

a league of her own

RW

oh what a wonderful honeymoon

in 1950 your dad gave me
a hundred dollar bill
for my wedding outfit

mama and i drove to s.w. anderson's
in owensboro where i bought
a light blue two piece gabardine suit

plus low heel shoes a purse and
a pretty hat all with navy trim
i weighed 95 pounds

your dad wore a 2 tone brown and tan
jacket with khaki pants brown shoes
and no hat we got married in utica

on a saturday at the preacher's house
his wife was our witness
your dad had his own car

a black 1949 chevy fleetline 4 door deluxe
it looked like a gangster car
after our wedding we drove

to the most lovely little cabin
off highway 60 a few miles outside owensboro
where we met our best friends

margie romans and ralph boyd
who had gotten married earlier
the same day in centertown

each couple had our own room
and bathroom oh what a wonderful honeymoon
your dad had to be at work early

monday morning he was such a hard worker
always devoted to his job he started working
at the mines when he was 16

oh what a wonderful honeymoon

GRW

ronnie paige

i loved being pregnant
i was excited about thanksgiving

early that morning when my water broke
huge flakes of snow started falling
the wind picked up

my contractions grew hard and fast
we drove through howling wind and heavy snow
and lightning and thunder it was a blizzard

going down hoover hill it was too dangerous
to slow down or stop so with mouths open
we watched the headlights of a car

slide off the narrow road then disappear
headed towards the ravine
at the owensboro hospital

on thursday november 23rd 1950 at 2:18pm
on thanksgiving day you were born
ronnie paige

i was so happy
as you took your first drink
of milk from my breast

i heard your dad
down the hall
yell with joy

he was so excited
to have a new baby boy
we were so happy

back then they kept you
at the hospital for a week
when you had a baby

GRW

Your Dad's Badge

I still have it.

Here's why and how your Dad starting wearing a Badge. There was some meanness going on in Centertown, at The Horse Show. Sheriff Lawrence Westerfield called your Dad. They were friends. Lawrence asked your Dad to be his Deputy. Your Dad loved that job. Loved it too much. He was giving that, being Deputy Sheriff, more attention than I liked. I got to thinking about the fun he was having hanging out at Gene Bennett's Garage with his friends. I wanted to go to a movie or eat out. We lived in town close to the garage so one night I walked over there. I opened the door and looked at Ed standing there tall and handsome. I went over to him and ripped the Badge off his shirt. I wish I could remember what happened after that. Maybe I can't remember because the next day you boys and I walked to the grocery with our dog Rags. Rags ran out in front of a car. I picked him up and took him back to our yard. We talked with him as he lay dying. Rags was the first of so many of your dogs that were lost to the highway.

GRW

3 dead peckers

old man cherry and spadge and otley
sat whittling smoking hand rolled cigarettes
solving the problems of the world
the mysteries of the universe mid summer
on the rickety old rainbow bread bench
in front of maddox's general store
centertown kentucky when roberta
raced by giving all 3 men the evil eye
in the store she remarked to glen
the owner pointing she said
there sit 3 dead peckers
glen grinned but clamped
his erupting guffaw
when roberta and her groceries
departed glen mosied out front
and shared roberta's words with
old man cherry and spadge and otley

the first responder was old man cherry
who said well i hope she comes back
in spring when the sap is running

RW

The Entertainer

You kids loved outdoor drive-in movies. When we couldn't go to one I put our small t.v. in the window facing the yard. It was black and white. There were no color ones yet so I put blue or yellow tin paper over the screen. I put out chairs or a quilt and made popcorn. I loved entertaining you kids.

GRW

No Greater Love

I know not everyone feels this way
But I have to say that there's
No greater love
Than a mother's love for her children

I'm blessed to have six children
All still living and in good health
I loved being pregnant
And giving birth to each one

I loved watching them grow up
And being there for them
Ronnie Paige born November 23, 1950
Bradford Alan, born December 5, 1952

Paddy Baker, born August 21, 1955
Edwina Drew, born August 25, 1957
Robin Render, born November 29, 1960
Velvet Dawn, born July 2, 1962

I'm proud of and thankful for
Each and every one
I'm 82 years old now
I'll soon be joining my loving husband Ed

I know that not everyone feels this way
But I have to say that there's
No greater love
Than a mother's love for her children

GRW

To Our Six Babies

I felt your first move inside my belly
I was excited felt your feet in my ribs practicing
Wanting to be born

The water flows your cord is cut
Then a sweet cry and tiny fingers
Clinging to my breast

Your Dad shouting down the hall
Proud

Love, Mama

GRW

Bloomer Joined the Circus

Now back to living in the Algonquin Park area in the chicken house. Before we moved from Centertown our Dad's friend Bloomer English left his family and joined the circus. Bloomer worked at the mines awhile, where your Dad worked. Bloomer's wife, Gracie, asked him to get her a bucket of water. He did but when he didn't come back she went looking and found the bucket close to the well. But no Bloomer.

He joined up with The Barnum & Bailey Circus to work with the elephants. In Louisville Daddy took us to the Park where Barnum & Bailey wintered their animals. We went in the building and there was Bloomer with the elephants.

GRW

Precious Memories

As we sit by the fire and reminisce
And look at old photographs so dear
I think of all the things I dearly miss
With my little ones who were so near

I recall the first words they said
The first steps they took all alone
I remember their prayers as they knelt by their beds
And the love that makes a house a home

You would think you couldn't go another day
With troubles and burdens to bear
With their cuts and scratches from hours of play
They came running to me for tender loving care

The weariness would leave as the day went by
Because of the sweet things they said
I would turn my head and hide the tears
And I would send them out to play

With six healthy children we have been blessed
Each one in their own wonderful way
Would make or draw something of their best
And surprise me on Mother's Day

Years have passed and our children are grown
But the happiness they brought us remains
We look forward to the day they all come home
But our home will never be the same

GRW

our first our last our next kiss

in 1949 we fell in love
oh our first kiss
your warm oh so kissable lips
in the front seat
of your black chevy
fleetline 4 door deluxe
we embraced
our first kiss

60 years later still in love
oh our last kiss
your warm oh so kissable lips
were growing cold as you sat
in your recliner by the window
in our beaver dam living room
i kissed you 12 times
we embraced
our last kiss

it's 2015 now i'm 83 and still in love
oh our next kiss
your warm oh so kissable lips
with all my heart i await

we shall again embrace
our next kiss

GRW

the night watch

i lifted my wind up alarm clock
from under my army cot
i was excited to have my own room
the long kitchen closet
as i stared at the baseball cards and pennant flags
tacked to the wood slat wall
i heard mama gently singing a sweet gospel song
i looked up to see her ironing clothes
there were clothes on hangers hangers hangers
and a waist high pile yet to go
the clock said 10:47pm

the night watch

i heard a truck crunching gravel on our long driveway
then 4 loud knocks on our blue front door
when mama opened the door 3 men stepped in
one said we need ed
daddy had slipped green khaki work pants
over his boxer shorts no shirt on
the upset man excitedly explained that
someone had been shot and
others beat up on the picket line

we need your help ed he said
the clock said 3:14am

the night watch

screaming tires screeching metal shattering glass
yet another wreck in front of our old farmhouse
on foggy nights folks missed the stop sign
where gravel road and asphalt road collide
peering out the front window i saw the rear end
of a car smoke and fire and a bloody face
with arms trying to crawl out of the gully across the road
racing out the front door daddy yelled stay here
the clock said 2:38am

the night watch

the telephone rang out in the night
mama answered she said ed it's the sheriff
yes daddy was a farmer and a coal miner
but he was also ohio county deputy sheriff
when the sheriff had a problem that was too tough
he called daddy who strapped on his holster and
loaded pistol put on his badge and cowboy hat and
said somebody's been hurt i'll take care of it go back to bed
the clock said 1:23am

the night watch

my eyes popped open as roy orbison
cranked all the way up
and another voice that sounded familiar yelled
ed bet you can't catch us then
as the jacked up red chevy nova revved its engine
i saw daddy slip out from the side of our house
he was in his boxer shorts no shirt
he had the pump action 12 gauge shotgun
which he aimed towards the car and
as he let out the howl of 10 madmen
the muscle car set fire to the road
keening teenagers moaning then screaming as
daddy unloaded the shotgun *kaboom kaboom kaboom*
blasting rounds skimming the top of the car he stood
now in the middle of the road as the scared kids fled
up the road and over the hill
with their hearts in their hands
the clock said 12:58am

the night watch

ed ed hey ed your bull's out
come on i'll help you get him back in
a man yells in the middle of the night
from somewhere out front
the front door slams
i didn't get up i stayed in bed
the clock said 4lordy08am

the night watch

the cedar wind whistled the pine wind whined
through the holes in the attic walls
my dead uncle ray visited me again a friendly spirit
stopping by to say hello and wish me well
dead relatives appeared often at the foot of my bed
in the attic room my brother and i shared
we had twin beds a lamp an am radio and
my wind up alarm clock on a night stand
the only furniture in our open raftered
unfinished floor bedroom the only place to walk
was from stairs to beds a vast open space
frequented by ghosts and singing winds
and my brother and me
it had snowed hard through the night
the house still moaned
i knew it was time to rise and shine i smelled bacon
mama was serving daddy breakfast i heard them talking
downstairs in the kitchen daddy was telling a joke
mama was laughing and i knew there would be no school
oh boy so i closed my eyes and stayed in bed
the clock said 5am

the night watch

RW

quilting in deep snow

i sat near the open fireplace
playing army with toy soldiers

as the red orange and yellow
wood fire snapped crackled and popped
i glanced to the snowflaked panes

through the frosted window
early january ice and snow
was whirling into a blizzard

the fresh coffee and cinnamon rolls
smelled delicious but suddenly
i was more interested in the story

mammie igleheart was sharing
with mamaw and aunt rena
and miss haddie and mama
as they quilted

my little reno was 4 years old
daddy had a wood shed at the end
of the yard where he kept dry wood
and the sharpest ax you have ever seen

one day reno got the ax out
and split his foot open
scared us all to death
i put medicine on his foot

and for days he was awful sick
blood poison developed in his body
and he died

he was so quiet and pretty
little blue pants and white shirt
and a tie like buster brown
tied in a bow

when he was so sick and dying
he said do you see those ladies
dancing up there and he was looking
straight up toward the ceiling

his death about killed me
and i was pregnant
with little ruthie
she was born the next month

then mammie igleheart stopped talking
and started sobbing crying hard
mama held her

the snow and ice fell harder
the fire crackled and popped louder

RW

the year granddaddy died

the year granddaddy died
i was 8 years old nearly 9

it was 1959 when he taught me
how to drive with my left knee

many years and miles i've traveled and
i still drive here there and everywhere

i'm still amazed at what can be done
when you know how to drive

with your left knee
i'm forever thankful for granddaddy

for teaching me how to drive
with my left knee

the year granddaddy died

RW

a master of checkers

on a snow drifting wind yelping wild nature kentucky
winter's night daddy said come on boys and we followed

me worrying about mama hoping she would be safe
left by herself there on the farm while we went to hang

out with the men at gene lee's centertown garage old
iron coal stove pay day candy bars small bottle coca

colas old man cherry and spadge tooley sitting on broke
down rigged up chairs with an upside down five gallon

bucket between them serving as table for checkers
the winner keeps playing as the other men take turns in

the loser's seat the old timers exchanging local gossip
and telling stories stories stories and i'm a shy boy at

least around these men but i'm forever listening to every
syllable watching each subtle nuance then the inevitable

questions are directed at me and daddy says speak up
ronnie and i respond with one line answers yet over a

decade of growing up winter nights at gene lee's
centertown garage sitting near the old iron coal stove

i too became a storyteller and
a master of checkers

RW

boys it's time to hoe

i'm 9 years old in early september 1959
home from a day in 4th grade with miss myrtle calvert

best teacher ever centertown school
my brother brad and i are playing pepper

in the front yard barehanded baseball
throwing hard as we can 1st one to drop the ball loses

our sisters paddy and edie
are playing with dolls when mama yells

from back of the house
boys it's time to hoe

our one acre garden and two acre orchard
are on the southside of the backyard

tween our yellow farmhouse and red barn
daddy will be home after 4 o'clock

so brad and i run to the barn
and get our sharpened hoes

paddy and edie beat us to the garden
they sit at the edge playing with dolls

brad and i are chopping and digging
out crabgrass when i hear a loud

rumbling and roaring i look up to see
an overloaded log truck driving too fast

flying down the hill i'm staring as it gets close
to the front of our house when a chain snaps

then in slow motion the most godawful
crash bam boom as logs fall from the truck

rolling over the road coming to rest
in our front yard i let out a deep sigh

glad us kids listened to mama yell
boys it's time to hoe

RW

wrestling hercules

daddy was a mighty man a warrior the best
he never lost a fight he defeated all the rest

there's a super 8 video somewhere
that mama shot of my brother brad and me

wrestling hercules yes to me
daddy was and will always be hercules

one of daddy's brothers was a sniper in korea
a green beret then later became an agent for the cia

one day when i complimented him on being
such a badass he looked me in the eyes

and said no not me it was your dad who was
the badass he taught us all there was to know

bout how to be tough he never lost a fight
and he was in plenty and during the depression

our dad jasper gave ed one shotgun shell
a day to bring home meat for the table

so my friends when i say i was raised by
a 10th degree badass a 10th degree smartass

know that i'm not kidding the 1st 17 years
of my life would make marine boot camp

look like the training school for valet parking
and that's nothing against the marines

or valet parkers daddy taught me how to be
a warrior how to fight relentlessly i saw him

get into several fights and yes he won them all
and oh daddy could tell jokes and stories

for days and nights without repeating himself
he was a good neighbor if anyone needed

help on a farm or at the mines daddy was
the go to guy and at home when daddy was

in good spirits he liked to wrestle and box
my brother brad and i tried many times

to wrestle him to the ground but we never
could he always won in the super 8 video

wrestling match daddy ripped the rear end
out of his work pants his boxer shorts are shining

daddy was a mighty man a warrior the best
he never lost a fight he defeated all the rest

wrestling hercules

RW

the boxer

"A champion is someone who gets back up even when he can't."
Jack Dempsey

i've been down so low the ground looked up
failure has been my greatest success

daddy was a boxer
the fiercest of them all

he never lost a fight
he taught me how to take a punch a punch

and another punch always watching
for the opening then fast as lightning

jab jab jab kaboom daddy was a boxer
he taught me how to fight

he taught me how to fight through pain
ignoring blood sweat and tears

to never give up no matter what
to keep fighting so i became a boxer

unlike daddy i've lost more fights than i've won
but daddy taught me to never give up

that life is rarely fun
time and time and time again

i hit rock bottom with nowhere left to go
many times i stood alone

abandoned by everyone but mama
no matter what she never left my corner of the ring

so every time i failed
slowly surely i found a way to rise again

a rocky rugged mountain
is my body now

a poet from kentucky
with a gentle soul

miles and miles i've traveled many fights i've fought
oh the story of my life

despite the losses
against all odds

relentlessly leaning into the wind
without regrets i remain

the boxer
       RW

if it be your will dear god
please help me grow

in yet another moment of darkness
i confessed to mama

i said mama i don't think i'll ever
get any taller than i am now you see

i was 5 feet 4 inches tall for at least
a thousand years and i was worried sick

that i'd never get any taller so
one sad morning i shared my troubled

mind with mama she said well ronnie paige
why don't you pray about it

and so i prayed and i prayed and i prayed
and lo and behold the summer between

my junior and senior year of high school
i started having godawful pains in all my joints my bones

and the next thing i knew my prayers
were answered as i shot up from

5 feet 4 inches to 6 feet plus an inch tall
so when i started my final year

of high school age 16 i was
one happily relieved young man and yes

dear friends believe me when i say
i do believe in the power of prayer

if it be your will dear god please help me grow

RW

Moxley and Eirene
Moonshine King Burgoo Queen

Mama gave me a tin cup when I was a boy. Til I left home, when I was 17, I wore a thin rope, to hold my pants up. I've always been skinny. I kept my tin cup, and a knife with a bottle opener, on my rope. They both came in handy many times including, and especially, my last visit with Moxley and Eirene.

I was 16, a year away from leaving home, leaving home for good, leaving home forever. I'd come to visit Moxley and Eirene, travelin by boat, alone. I didn't know how many more times I'd have this opportunity. It was a crisp clear day in early September. The sad and glad of early fall filled me up. It felt good but it ached with loneliness too.

Some of you know that several miles southwest of Centertown, 27 miles from Owensboro, Owensboro, the self-proclaimed burgoo capitol of the world, deep, and I mean deep, in the bottoms where the bobcats still live, on an island on a tight curve of Green River, the deepest river in the world, with catfish that have swallowed children whole, the Green River, with nests of water moccasins in every cove, on a tight curve of Green River lived, in a wicked, crooked dirt hut old Moxley and his wife Eirene. The island, called Toad's Island, rose, peaking with a small hill, above the Green. It had flooded only once, back in '37.

Unlike most of the Irish and Scots in Ohio County, the fifth largest county, and one of the poorest, in Kentucky, home of Bill Monroe, the father of Bluegrass music, resting across the Green River from Muhlenberg County and Paradise, unlike most of the Irish and Scots Moxley's parents had come from Hungary and Eirene's from Greece back in the 1800's.

When I was a boy I visited Moxley and Eirene with Daddy or Granddaddy Dick. We stopped by after runnin trot lines. Some city people might call them trout lines but we never caught no trout on them: we caught catfish, snappin turtles, snakes and eels all of which occasionally found their way into Eirene's burgoo, the best, and most peculiar, unlike any other, burgoo in the world. Eirene was the burgoo queen. Although few will admit it, folks from miles away, including all the way from Owensboro, eventually found their way to Toad's Island, down on the Green River, and borrowed the recipes, which continue to be used on rare, private, and special occasions, for Eirene's burgoo and Moxley's moonshine whiskey. Moxley was the moonshine king.

Moxley and Eirene had an orchard and a garden but Moxley always said he lived on snake, snappin turtle, possum, and moonshine whiskey. By the time I was 16 I'd seen him eatin and drinkin all of them more than once and with his big red and purple nose I figured he was tellin the truth. He kept his moonshine still right in front of their hut. They had a one-eyed black cat with no tail called Spit and a three-legged dog called Tick.

Eirene, I guessed, was probably a witch but a decent one and by the time I first met her, when I was a boy, she may have forgotten most of what she once knew. But she had remembered how to make burgoo, the most unusual and distinctively flavored burgoo I've ever tasted. Same was true of Moxley's moonshine. I can barely even approximate their magic recipes. I was a poor witness especially once Moxley began offerin pourin his moonshine, God's Tears, into my tin cup. It was the smoothest hard liquor I've ever, in my entire life, tasted. My vision blurred as I watched Moxley on my left and Eirene on my right. Sometimes they became one, not too pretty, person. But, despite their strangeness, I always liked both of them so no matter how ugly they looked as one person it didn't matter, I didn't care, I just sat there watchin and grinnin and smellin while they brewed the burgoo and the moonshine.

Moxley poured in spring water which he collected runnin directly out of the side of their Toad's Island hill. He added pure cane sugar, cracked corn and malt. He always cut the first gallon with water cause it was so strong. It kicked harder than a mule or an udder sore milk cow. Sometimes he added burnt sugar and water to change the colorin. He did that for variety. While Moxley was cookin up his strange brew my attention wandered back and forth so I watched Eirene cook her burgoo too.

I watched her make burgoo several times, over the years, and it was always different dependin on what she had available. This particular time, the last time I saw her make it, when I was 16, she killed a chicken, snuck up behind it and cut its head off before it knew what happened, then she plucked it and tossed it in, then instead of beef or pork, she added chunks of snappin turtle, possum, water moccasin, and eel. Even though fish isn't common to burgoo I'm pretty sure, despite the moonshine I'd drunk, that she threw in several pieces of catfish.

I'd brought her two rabbits I killed huntin with Daddy. I helped her skin them then she threw them in, bones and all, didn't even cut off their heads. Of course the pot, which was on an open fire in front of the hut, was filled with water from the river. She also mixed in some dirty dish water. For some reason I never discovered, before addin the water she first placed river rocks in the bottom of the pot. Once the water was ready she tossed in tomatoes, potatoes, onions, garlic, cabbage, peppers, carrots, corn, beans, peas, ketchup, salt, pepper, thyme, vinegar, sauces, homemade red wine, plenty of Moxley's moonshine, pinches of a variety of herbs, then she said words I didn't understand, maybe Greek, the language of her ancestors, and she said them like she was castin a spell.

It was spooky the way she chanted those words gettin a glazed faraway look in her dark eyes. Good Lord I knew it was gonna be good. It always was. She cooked it for hours. I'm not sure how many hours cause I passed out.

When I woke up the sun had set. It was a beautiful starry night. The full moon was risin. A pack of wild dogs was barkin way off in the distance, up river. Crickets, katydids, frogs, and lightnin bugs brightened the night providin a brilliant sound and light show.

Eirene and Moxley handed me food and drink, burgoo and moonshine, best food in the world, bar none. We stayed up late, into the night, sharin stories, listenin close to each other, to the bobcat's mournful wail, listenin to the spirits walkin the earth late, late at night when the vail tween worlds disappears.

The next mornin, just after daybreak, a buzzin fly woke me up. All three of us had fallen asleep on the ground, up close to the fire which had fallen to a dull ember, almost out. The sun was crackin the sky over the trees east of the Green. I rose, walked silently to my boat and glided away. It was my final visit, the last time I saw my dear ancient friends Moxley and Eirene, moonshine king burgoo queen.

RW

mama's little helper

daddy was a coal miner
for 43 years he worked for peabody coal company

daddy was a union man
for 43 years he was a member of the u.m.w.a.

the united mine workers of america
provided the best health insurance anyone

could find in the impoverished back country
farm and coal mine lands of western kentucky

we all liked dr. bennett he was our family doctor
dr. bennett's office was in beaver dam

mama knew and practiced all the old and natural ways
of healing and treating sickness illness and disease

but health insurance and doctor prescribed medicine
was the new modern suggested way of doing things

so there came a point in my growing up years
when mama practiced both the old and the new

ways of healing sickness illness and disease
mama loved me so much more than anyone

so whatever mama asked me to do i did
and i did whatever mama asked me to do

without question or hesitation cause i knew
mama loved me so when mama said take this

no matter what it was i took it when mama said
take this pill i took it cause i knew it meant

that mama loved me i always did what mama said
then the 60s came along i loved the hippies

down on the farm i read everything about the hippies
i could get my hands on so eventually inevitably

i became a hippie and you know what
the hippies loved to take pills

yes one pill made me larger and one pill made me small
how do i know you ask i know cause i took them all

anytime someone said take this i did especially
if it was a pill cause i knew mama loved me

and mama gave me pills so whenever a hippie friend
said take this i knew they loved me too

so i always took the little pill well i took many little pills
my friends the years have flown by now i'm 63
a hippie i remain

jinn and i are married i'm happy as can be
jinn is a genius she gives me the right herbs

it's strange the deep sense of love i feel
when jinn says ron please take one of these pills

i've always liked the old the natural ways
herbal medicines and health aids energy and libido

boosters are the best well yes i've taken
quite a few chemicals but i prefer herbs

nature's way is the best
mama's little helper

RW

old blue

mama knew i loved to adventure
so when my farm work was done

mama let me roam
i loved to wander with family and friends

but when no one was around
i'd yell for old blue and we'd head out on our own

a half mile down the road from home
old blue and i stepped from gravel to brown grass

then into waist high orange sagebrush we
meandered round tall leafless oak trees we

paused to listen as wind sang in the evergreens
old blue smelled everything we balanced unsteadily

on the half gone log bridge old blue fell into the creek i
kept an eye out for movements near and far

old blue shook himself dry we came out
of the woods and headed up the hill

that overlooked our rolling farm three fourths
of the way up before the next tree line i

found a mossy spot in the sagebrush
old blue followed the scent of a rabbit he'd

already entered the forest but seeing me
he returned and sniffed out his own soft

spot then we nestled down ready for an afternoon
nap old blue fell fast asleep i stared up at the turquoise

sky and watched as a solitary white cloud shapeshifted
momentarily blocking the sun then

out of nowhere a crow
entered the cloud and as i drifted

to sleep with old blue by my side i wondered if
the crow was lost and would it come out alive

mama knew i loved to adventure
mama let me roam

RW

i hate suckering tobacco

on a hot sunny september morning i put the top down
on my 1991 red miata today i'm driving to beaver dam

to visit mama we all worked hard on our old kentucky
    farm
i leave my highlands hermitage drive up cherokee road

pass bellarmine university where i taught for a couple of
    years
the thomas merton center holds works i published by
    merton

and robert lax james laughlin ron seitz and lawrence
    ferlinghetti
i cut over to dixie highway head up muldraugh hill through
    fort knox

hang a right at tip top ah kentucky backroads barns and
    open fields
through irvington hardinsburg mcquady fordsville dundee
    hartford

then beaver dam but it's not the small towns on those old
kentucky backroads it's the farms the barns the fields

that's where and when the memories come flooding in
i see the farmers cutting yellowing ripe for harvest tobacco

some of the barns already full i hated suckering tobacco
it was the worst job of them all suckers are little tobacco
   plants

they grow where stalk and leaf meet with mama's help
my brother brad and i pulled the small suckers by hand

cut the large ones with razor sharp buck knives we wore
work gloves because the tobacco juice is sticky as honey

it's hot as hell no wind at all in between the mile long rows
suckering takes longer than forever but when it's finally
   done

we top we cut the pretty flowers out of the top of the tall
tobacco plants with topping done it's time to cut the tall
   plants

down with our lethal tobacco knives which are actually
   hatchets
now that's fun but be careful or lose your life before
   cutting

though we drop tobacco sticks the same sticks we built
   forts
with when we were young we drop them at every 7th
   plant

then we cut laying 7 plants into one big pile then when we
   reach
the end of the row go back and spear the stalks onto the
   sticks

then let the tobacco sit in the patch for a handful of days
let it dry then pull trailer with tractor load it up then hang

it in the barn then mid-winter hopefully before Christmas
on a cold misty morning when the leaves are soft and
    moist

take it down and strip leaves from stalks tie them in knots
according to size then load them on the truck and take
    them

to the owensboro tobacco market hoping for top dollar
then when they finally sell no matter the month well
    christmas

has finally come my brother and i with our hard work we
    had won
the freedom to buy our own clothes a new tv a record
    player

and even a motorcycle boy did we ever have fun
there's so much involved in growing tobacco a farmer's
    work

is never done well i started at the end but know this that
not long after we sold our tobacco when winter was nearly
    over

we piled up wood for a bonfire we burnt off ground for
    our next
crop we planted seeds in our new tobacco bed

farming is an honorable and a rewarding life
but from droughts floods rain snow the farmer must defend

i left the farm at 17 but when i drive those old backroads
i'm on the farm a country boy again

RW

song of the auctioneer

buy all that for one money folks
song of the auctioneer

will someone pay 30 for these
one of a kind watercolor kits from the 60s
who'll pay 30 dollars
do i hear 5
5 right here
do i hear 6
6 right here
do i hear 8
8 right here
do i hear 10
10 right here
do i hear 12
12 right here
do i hear 15
15 do i hear 15
12 right here
do i hear 15
15 do i hear 15
sold for 12
to this gentleman
number 23

buy all that for one money folks
song of the auctioneer

on a sunny september day
when i was 9 years old
i went with mama and daddy
to the auction of old man ashby's estate
outside centertown in the country off matanzas road
old man ashby was a family friend
he was real old when he died
he was well to do and
he was a collector
so was i

buy all that for one money folks
song of the auctioneer

i love auctions
went to them whenever i could
song of the auctioneer
made my heart sing
i liked to get there early
so i could look over everything and decide
what i wanted to bid on and
what i could afford to buy
i loved civil war and indian artifacts
at old man ashby's auction i got lucky
i bid on and bought a civil war sword and
an indian spear and a huge canvas wallet

of indian arrowheads somebody in the family
still has all of them not sure who
i've gotten rid of nearly everything i once owned
gave nearly of it away i love to give gifts

buy all that for one money folks
song of the auctioneer

on this sunny september day
i'm 63 years old
my wife jinn and i went
to big al's auction in clarksville indiana
big al decided to go fishing for a while
maybe live in his truck on the road
big al's a good guy
he was a collector
so was i

buy all that for one money folks
song of the auctioneer

i love auctions
hadn't been to one in years and years
i got out bid on the davy crockett wood rocking horse
and the turquoise handled texas ranger cap pistol
but i won the bidding for those
one of a kind watercolor kits from the 60s
with 2 prim english children riding
a tin rocket ship to the moon

jinn watched the moon landing from her mother's navel

buy all that for one money folks
oh i love auctions and

the song of the auctioneer

RW

in kentucky

in kentucky
when i was a boy growing up

on a wild nature backwoods farm
on a warm september late afternoon

i bridled our big work horse
and rode bareback

out of the barn
down the meadow

across the fields
heading to the woods

the horse with a mind of his own
going faster and faster

and when we reached the creek
he jumped high and long

and i went sailing
flying flying off his back

and when i landed
my head hit a big limestone rock

and for a lightning fast instant
i saw stars then passed out

when i came to
it was almost dark

the horse was gone
i walked back to the barn

swearing i'd put that damn
saddle on next time

RW

stevie fell out

there were more than 20 of us piled crammed
squeezed front and back i was sitting on

mama's lap my brother brad was sitting
on my lap granddaddy dick was at the wheel

speeding up matanzas road to centertown
when the old ford swerved in the sharp

crow nose curve the back passenger door
popped open and stevie fell out when

granddaddy dick finally heard the backseat
voices yelling then screaming steve fell out

stevie fell out the tires burned rubber skidding
as granddaddy dick slammed on the brakes

luckily it was autumn stevie brushed leaves
off his clothes and out of his hair as he

crawled out of the ditch then raced to the
car which he dove into head first thankful

to be alive and not left behind granddaddy
dick yelled somebody hold on to that boy

as tires squealed burning rubber again
the car filled with several generations

flew into the night

RW

arriving

not many deer crossed the road back then
but life was wild i remember the call

october 1959 i was nearly 9 mama was
in the house on the phone i could hear her

crying moaning talking i was standing behind
the barn it was hotter than hot i started praying

for granddaddy to live to be all right i was just
a boy but granddaddy was special to me real

special he was wild like the deer that appeared
and vanished when granddaddy drove 90 miles

per hour on highway 261 between fordsville
and hardinsburg heading from centertown to

valley station going home me riding shotgun
windows down flying on old kentucky country

backroads so many times granddaddy stopped
at a little grocery near rough river to get me

soda crackers and ginger ale cause back then
i got car sick but granddaddy only laughed and

smiling talked to me like i was real and not just
a kid i remember a 6 pack of beer on the floor

in the back and a pint of whiskey in the glove
box granddaddy was real when he breathed

the earth breathed he moved things he was
a grader operator building the watterson

expressway around louisville he was a barber
he cut hair he made records he traveled and

sang on radio stations and at concerts he
yodeled he cleared the land the rundown

farm he bought that had belonged to his
mom and dad my greatgrandparents render

he went fox and coon hunting with his friends
in the middle of the night always drinking

whiskey and telling stories that made the men
laugh i know cause i went with him whenever

i was allowed granddaddy dick didn't preach but
his life was a sermon he was spirit holy spirit

no matter what anyone says so i drive fast
with the windows down and i don't wear a seat belt

and i'm taking a hard curve with the long wind
and the tall green trees and the turquoise sky

and the energy comes to me and it fills me and
i feel what granddaddy felt the energy of life of sex

of love of family of longing and i smile and i cry
on this hot august morn and i know that somehow

granddaddy's spirit is still here with me and my
head and my body want to explode but i hold

on to the wheel with all my might moving from
day into night and back to light finally finally

arriving

RW

the dance

we wear these garments
dwell in these temples

briefly we are
short lived temporary

sun worshippers we
are delicate pale

pink blossoms on
van gogh's almond tree

our fine attire covering
bones dancing bones

the bones of life
loving bones

bones in love
the dance

a waltz fragrant
spring wind carries

us to the end
of the night

RW

a week before Christmas

a week before Christmas. the first night in a month Daddy didn't have to work a double shift at the coal mine. Daddy and Mama piled us kids into the back of our old Chevrolet and we drove 30 miles from our western Kentucky farm, outside Centertown, in Ohio County, where Bill Monroe birthed bluegrass music, all the way to Owensboro, in Daviess County, where they had the last public hanging in the United States. i was born in Owensboro. so was my brother Brad, and my 4 sisters Paddy & Edie & Robin & Velvet. so was Johnny Depp.
Daddy drove us through the rich neighborhoods to look at the Christmas lights. wow! what electric colored splendor shining on a cold Kentucky night. us kids ooohed and aaahhhed in awe of the beauty.
then Daddy drove on to Sears, in downtown Owensboro, where we did our Christmas shopping. Daddy and Mama made us kids stay far away from them while they shopped for us. us kids had each saved enough money to buy Mama and Daddy Christmas gifts. how exciting! Christmas is still my favorite holiday. i especially love the blue lights. blue is my favorite color. yesterday i bought a strand of 100 blue lights for $4.99 and strung them across the ceiling of my hermitage. welcome Christmas, my favorite holiday of the year.

RW

Mama and Daddy Taught Me

Mama and Daddy taught me, through actions more than words, to never look up to or down at anyone that we're all in this together, eyeball to eyeball, shoulder to shoulder. no matter what is going on around me that's how i choose to live my life.

RW

The Sound of Snowflakes
on Christmas Eve

1962. School was out for Christmas break. I was 12.
A little before dark, snow started falling.

It snowed all night.

Brad and I slept in the unfinished attic. Through the
   night
I listened to winter's wind whistling through the cracks

in our attic walls. I listened to winter's wind weaving
songs accompanied by the cedar and pine trees

surrounding and protecting our home.
Before daybreak I heard Mama and Daddy downstairs.

Daddy loading the furnace with coal then going out the
back door headed to the barn to feed the animals. Mama

in the kitchen cooking breakfast. She was singing,
   quietly,
"Oh Christmas Tree." I smelled bacon and biscuits and

gravy and coffee. Yes I was already drinking coffee.
Started when I was 6.

I woke Brad up. Brad was a sound sleeper. I said, "Hey, Brad, wake up. Let's go see how much snow we got. Hey, get

up. We've got to go milk the cows, chop the ice on the pond, and bring the coal in. Come on, Mama's cooking

breakfast. I'm going down."
Brad and I had breakfast with Mama and Daddy. As

always Mama's cooking was delicious. We ate every crumb. Brad licked his plate.

Daddy left for work at the mines.
After Brad and I finished our morning chores I got my

.410 shotgun and went hunting.
It had snowed over a foot during the night and giant

flakes were still falling. The snow wasn't letting up.
I walked and walked and walked. I was in awe of the

beauty, all the beauty that surrounded me.
I lost track of time.

I found myself in a field surrounded by woods. All around me the wind whispered through the limbs

the branches of the barren trees. The wind whispered through the fur of the evergreen trees. A lone crow

cawed in the distance, searching its way home.
It was then I realized that I was hearing a sound

louder than any other, a loud but gentle and soft
sound, the sound of falling snowflakes.

That sound, that moment, comes back to me often,
including now, transporting me to a time and a

place long gone, but a time and a place that will
live eternally in me in my heart's memory.

RW

the old singing barn

arm in arm we stand
in front of the old Rosine barn
the father of bluegrass music Bill Monroe
his old homeplace Jerusalem Ridge
his grave not far away
arm in arm creative warriors we stand
in this pioneer Kentucky promised land
rugged dangerous terrible beauty

where diamonds are created
arm in arm we stand in Kentucky
the promised land New Jerusalem
in Kentucky we persevere we never give up
and as the father of bluegrass Bill Monroe
and his Band of Angels watch and listen

the creative imagination in this Kentucky
where diamonds are created promised land
the creative imagination is the doorway
to spiritual realms arm in arm united we stand
we dwell in Kentucky we dwell in the realms
of the creative imagination shaman poets
nabi prophet ancient timeless lightning poets we be
no 9 to 5 for us every rhythmed moment

every rhythmic heartbeat every drop of lifeblood
    energy
we devote to being pure channels of divine
creative imagination we are servant vessels sacred
flutes for Great Spirit Holy Ghost gladly devotedly
doing all we can to uplift inspire comfort heal
awaken with all the creative arts awaken and

help make the world a better place in which to be
we refuse to believe it's too late for healing
if we screwed it up we can clean it up
and I see The Dalai Lama looking deep into my eyes
and I hear him say "it's okay to be happy" then laughing
as only The Dalai Lama can laugh
and here we are arm in arm at the old singing barn
with Bill Monroe and his Band of Angels watching
    listening

as Elizabeth Maines as County Line's J. B. Miller
as Mama and my aunt Jo Carolyn The Render Sisters
gifted all angelically gifted sing sing
sing the old songs and yes poemed singing

poemed singing is the language of angels
a gift music is a gift to us humans
a gift to us from the angels from oh Great Spirit
our souls dwelling briefly in these templed bodies
life this opportunity to grow our souls life
a fleeting moment here now now gone gone gone
and I dedicate our show to Daddy who
just crossed over I dedicate our show to the strongest
    best man

I've ever known to Daddy who just crossed over as we
   all will
each at our appointed time and as Elizabeth
and J. B. and Mama and Jo sing
"When They Cut Down the Old Pine Tree"
and "Paradise" and "Walking after Midnight"
and "Will the Circle Be Unbroken" and

"Kentucky Waltz" and "Bury Me along the Big Sandy"
and I read "on parting" and Mama tells her
ice storm story bout the two pine trees
in the front yard being blown down in the
middle of last winter's ice stormed night and the big
   boom
they made and with tears in her eyes adding
the part bout Daddy then singing "When They Cut
   Down
the Old Pine Tree" to her then telling her

"I love you" and in my entire life I hardly ever
heard Daddy sing so now I'm doing everything in my
   power
to hold myself together and I'm remembering
how much my farmer coal miner Daddy
loved poems and stories and songs
and suddenly I hear other voices singing yes yes I hear
Bill Monroe and his Band of Angels and Daddy joining
   in

on the singing and precious memories fill me fill us
fill the old singing barn overflowing overwhelming
and my heart breaks wide open and a river of tears

a river of poemed heartblood souldrenched singing
   tears flows
and I'm filled with the epiphanied awareness that
like our ancestors we are our ancestors
we always have been will always be our ancestors and
   ourselves
all one we be our ancestors our lineage long creative
   strong

and arm in arm we stand
in front of this old weathered singing western Kentucky
   barn
and we hold on we stand arm in arm we stand united
we stand surrounded by with family friends allies
   guides angels
seen and unseen a host a global universal
non-violent creative spiritual shaman bodhisattva
   warrior army one we be

and arm in arm we hold on we never give up
there's more much more for us to do
our best poems gestating
on the way yet to come
new fires new storms new poems stories songs
the poemed storm generation
is birthed
newly born

so arm in arm
diamonds we stand
in front of this old singing barn

this weathered yet still standing singing western
    Kentucky barn
ancient we are still singing poems arm in arm united we
    stand
the storm generation newly born

RW

Thanksgiving in Kentucky

Mama and Daddy are here in the kitchen with Mama's parents, Mamaw and Granddaddy, and some of their kids, my aunts and uncles: Adeline, Kendall, Linda, Becky, Donna, Danny Boy, Stevie, and Timmy plus my brother Brad and our sisters Paddy and Edie. Edie's just four months old. It's Thanksgiving. I turned seven today. Daddy's home from the mines. Thanksgiving Day. My Louisville relatives are visiting. I'm excited by all the family energy by the laughing the loud conversations the singing. We love music. There are many singers and musicians in our family. Mama and Granddaddy are singing When They Cut Down the Old Pine Tree. Granddaddy is playing the ukulele. Daddy asks me to recite the Trees poem. In certain situations I'm shy but I finally find the courage.

Trees by Joyce Kilmer

I think that I shall never see
A poem lovely as a tree.

A tree whose hungry mouth is prest
Against the earth's sweet flowing breast;

A tree that looks at God all day,
And lifts her leafy arms to pray;

A tree that may in Summer wear
A nest of robins in her hair;

Upon whose bosom snow was lain;
Who intimately lives with rain.

Poems are made by fools like me.
But only God can make a tree.

I spend most of my time in nature and feel close kinship with trees so I memorized the Trees poem right after I first read it. Everyone is clapping and yelling. The kitchen is full of family. People fill the two doors, one leading to the utility room and the other to the living room. They're leaning in, looking over shoulders, to see and hear. I turn to Daddy. Do Hiawatha I say. I love that poem and I love to hear Daddy recite it.

"The Song of Hiawatha"
part XXII

Hiawatha's Departure

By the shore of Gitche Gumee,
By the shining Big-Sea-Water,
At the doorway of his wigwam,
In the pleasant Summer morning,
Hiawatha stood and waited,
All the air was full of freshness,
All the earth was bright and joyous,

> *And before him, through the sunshine,*
> *Westward toward the neighboring forest*
> *Passed in golden swarms the Ahmo,*
> *Passed the bees, the honeymakers,*
> *Burning, singing in the sunshine.*
> *Bright above him shone the heavens,*
> *Level spread the lake before him;*
> *From its bosom leaped the sturgeon,*
> *Sparkling, flashing in the sunshine;*
>
> *On its margin the great forest*
> *Stood reflected in the water,*
> *Every treetop had its shadow,*
> *Motionless beneath the water,*
> *From the brow of Hiawatha*
> *Gone was every trace of sorrow,*
> *As the fog from off the water,*
> *As the mist from off the meadow,*
> *With a smile of joy and triumph,*
> *With a look of exultation,*
> *As one who in a vision*
> *Sees what is to be, but is not,*
> *Stood and waited Hiawatha.*

Daddy knows the entire poem but he just recites the last section tonight cause it's a long poem and others are gonna sing and play. Everyone is spellbound by the music of the poem. I've seen tv and movie westerns but Hiawatha helps me look deeper into what I imagine the Indians are like. I wonder why they are called Indians. Who are they really like? This is a special moment here now listening to Daddy tell the poem, seeing everyone pay close attention listening to the story. I'm waking up to a new mystery, to many mysteries. I want to know about the lives of these strange people everyone called Indians. Why do I feel close to them?

I realize now that I'm a poet. My mind isn't sure what it means but my heart knows and that's enough for now. Daddy is a farmer and a coal miner. He's worked hard all his life for Peabody Coal Company and has never missed a day of work. He's the strongest hardest working man I've ever known. Daddy loves poetry. He knows many poems by heart. He encourages me to learn poems and I do. I already know quite a few. Daddy always asks me to do Word Power with him when the Reader's Digest arrives in the mail. Words, poems. The spirit in poetry brings Daddy and me close. My heart grows big. I hold back tears. I am thankful.

RW

loneliness

for decades now i've said that loneliness is
the most pervasive, and too often deadly, disease on the planet.

elitism is by far the worst, and most lethal, disease.

my parents taught me, through their actions and their words,
that we are all equal that we are all in this together. they taught me

to never look up to or down at anyone rather
eyeball to eyeball shoulder to shoulder. when i was a boy Mama

took us kids with her whenever she visited
the elderly the sick including rest homes. i've never experienced so

much loneliness as i have in rest homes.
Mama and Daddy taught us kids how to be good neighbors.

the only government for me
is the government of individual responsibility and being a good neighbor.

wherever i travel, down the street or to other countries,
i do my best to be friendly to say hello and thank you to
   pause to stop

for a little while and have even a brief conversation
   with folks
whether it be an old friend or someone i've just met

what happened to discourse to dialogue to
conversations to respectfully agreeing or disagreeing to
   being friends even

with those who are different, for whatever reason, than
   ourselves.
i believe in friendship.

RW

square bales ain't square and neither am i

any old farm girl or boy will tell you
square bales ain't square and neither am i

square bales are rectangular and wrapped with grass
   strings
a fractal i am i love to play with the math of poetry

i live in and beyond dimensions 1 and 2 and 3
oh the geometry of clouds and coastlines 2.78 and 3.14
   and 4.73

when i was a boy i made up poems and songs
i sang them as i walked across the fields

the 723rd bale of 125 pound wet bean hay weighs a ton
mama drove our 1010 john deere tractor

while my brother brad and i took turns
on the trailer then on the ground

loading in the field unloading at the barn
there's an art a dance a song to lifting and loading

125 pound rectangular bales of wet bean hay
use your legs and back and arms equally

cows love it but farm girls and boys
agree that the hardest work on the farm

in summer is hauling wet bean hay
growing up on a farm was a gift

i learned to work hard without complaining
i'm thankful for that now

if you happened to know me
when i was an old farm boy

you'll surely realize
square bales ain't square and neither am i

a fractal i am i love to play with the math of poetry
i live in and beyond dimensions 1 and 2 and 3

when i was a boy i made up poems and songs
i sang them as i walked across the fields

now i'm a man and i still sing
oh the geometry of clouds and coastlines 2.78 and 3.14
    and 4.73

RW

mourning my father

we were hard on each other
six years after his death
there are times
during the day
in the night
i am hard on him still
yet despite my echoing anger
i have always loved him
and there are times
in the night
during the day
when i am certain
he always loved me

RW

at the walton's creek graveyard

as you know so well
i'm the oldest of 13

in 1950 i was pregnant with you
my first born child

when my little sister susan
was stillborn

at the walton's creek graveyard
surrounded by generations

of family i cried and cried
praying for my little sister susan

hoping my heartbreak
wouldn't harm you

you've always had
a certain sadness

GRW

I Loved the Stage

My sister Jo & I started singing at funerals after folks heard us sing at our grandmother Render's 1951 funeral. Whenever we were called we'd sing whatever they requested. We'd stop our work at home and take all our kids with us. We hated to practice so we'd go over songs on the way to the funeral.

I had more nerve than Dick Tracy. When Ed & I went to the Big E the entertainers often called someone on stage and I would always go up, one time with Little Richard to dance the twist. Ed said, Greta I've never seen anyone like you.

I loved the stage.

GRW

HellFire and Brimstone Electric Chair Evangelist

1948. Daddy took us to hear this HellFire and Brimstone Evangelist Maurice Davies at an old school in Owensboro. The Evangelist always preached about the Electric Chair. There was an old Electric Chair next to him on the stage.

Before the sermon Jo and I looked the chair over. It made our hair stand up. Daddy asked Evangelist Davies if his girls, Jo and me, could sing at one of his WOMI Radio station broadcasts. The Evangelist said yes. So the next Saturday we did. Elizabeth Hoover played, or banged on, the piano for us. Daddy listened to us on the radio as he cut hair in his barber shop.

He was proud of us.

GRW

Turnip and Mink Christmas

Jo and I wanted Christmas money so we asked Daddy how we could make a few dollars. He said take his mink trap and go out of town to a certain ditch and set it. We did exactly what he said because we knew he was a good trapper. I love raw vegetables. On our way to set the mink trap Jo and I came upon a turnip patch. We pulled a couple and ate them. Then we set the mink trap but didn't catch one.

Daddy had sent off several nice mink furs to the market. It was getting close to Christmas so every day he said go check the mail box. Then two days before Christmas the check came. We shouted and shouted we were so excited. We decorated our tree with popcorn and wild berries. I got a coloring book and crayons. It didn't take much to satisfy me. I'm the same way now. All I need is a roof over my head and a bed to lay my body down on.

GRW

Dear President Reagan

April 14, 1987

Dear President Reagan,

Would you kindly accept an invitation to breakfast. I'll take you to the Centertown Restaurant where my husband and I and our friends meet every morning for coffee. Ten or more of us crowd around the table. First thing on the list to discuss is the weather then the sick in our community then a friend we lost. We discuss everything from the little things that happen at our home out on the country road to the big happenings at your house near the Hill. We discuss what industry might be taken from us next. We talk about the 32 coal miners who lost their jobs two weeks ago, the farmer who just auctioned off his machinery. We wonder if the hundreds of coal miners who lost their jobs in recent years will ever get called back to work. Today we were thankful that relatives and friends on set incomes of social security could stand in the cheese line again. Maybe you, Mr. President, can be here on a cheese giveaway day and stand in line with me when I get my mother's cheese for her.

Mr. President, I've lived in this small Ohio County western Kentucky community for 54 years. I love this little town and the people. We have three churches, a bank, a funeral chapel, a fire department, a city hall, a post office, a Masonic hall, two groceries, two garages, a bait shop, two beauty shops, a cafe, and a school for grades 1 through 8. A few years ago our school had a high school too but that was taken away. The Board of Education is going to take our elementary school away if we can't get more children enrolled. My mom went to school here. I went to school here. My children went to school here. My grandchildren are going to school here. This grand old school has sent out teachers, preachers, lawyers, engineers, nurses, doctors, and professors. When a school is taken out of a community, the community dies.

At the breakfast table they tell me that no matter what I do it won't help. The men say that even you Mr. President can't help. But I'm optimistic. I never say die. Help us Mr. President! Maybe you can send us an industry to put beside the Big River Power Plant which is a few miles down the road from here.

Mr. President, I sure hope to hear from you. Thank you for listening.

Sincerely,

Greta Render Whitehead
Rural Route #1
Centertown, Kentucky 42328

GRW

We Were All Thrifty in Those Days

In 1936 we lived in our Walton's Creek home. I went with our Mom and grandmother to the West Point school in Matanzas. There were huge bales of cotton being unloaded there, not far from the port at Green River. It was a WPA project for families who couldn't afford a mattress. I watched my Mom work hard putting one together. It was solid cotton covered with a strong stripe cloth. The old mattress we had was made of pounded straw or goose down. I always loved feather beds. They're so cozy.

One day Mama needed a few groceries so she sent my sister Jo Carolyn and me to Centertown. Two long miles for little girls to walk. Mama said we could get peppermint stick candy. On the way home a storm came up. I hovered over Jo because she was scared. Our groceries got wet and our candy wasn't as colorful but it was still good to eat.

Once we were at Aunt Sis's, in Matanzas, where we spent a lot of time. Aunt Sis needed washing powder so she sent my sister Jo Carolyn and our cousin Rex and me to Hagerman's big grocery store. She put an old hen in a grass sack so we could exchange it for the powder plus a few groceries. On the way to the store the hen laid an egg. We traded the egg for candy.

Jo and I did lunch room work, same as other kids. We had good food, dried beans and hot rolls. The older kids at our school were asked to gather scrap metal during the war. Us younger kids were asked to gather silk weed pods. Jo and I did that while the bigger kids, especially the boys, hauled in the scrap. If you've never opened a silk weed pod well you should. It's heavenly white and feels like silk. It was used to make parachutes for soldiers in the war. After the war my Aunt Sis bought an old parachute and made her daughter a wedding dress. It was beautiful. We were all thrifty in those days. My Mammie Igleheart would unravel an old dress and use the thread to create another handmade dress.

GRW

It Surely Says Heaven

Holding little sister's hand as we ran down the hillside toward the branch, our secret place, I turned and looked back at Mammie and Daddy Charlie's house and the little wooden gate we just passed through. It was heaven. So was the branch and the cool water running over our tiny toes. We peed in our pants and it didn't matter, it felt good.

We searched for rocks to make our buildings. Big and flat ones for the walls and roof. There were small red rocks, like crayons. We used these to mark the windows and doors. With our great imaginations we drew curtains on the windows.

Every now and then I stood on tip toes to see if the little wooden gate was open. Yes, heaven was still there. We went back to work, building the church for our little town. We made a path leading down to the water so we could drink and be baptized.

Time to check the wooden gate. I stood on my tip toes again and looked over the embankment. It was still there, the stone wall and the gate built by Daddy Charlie. I saw our angel Mammie washing clothes in the big iron kettle. Ah, I smelled the wood smoke and the lye soap she washed the clothes with. The sheets were white as snow. Oh Rock of Ages.

We looked at our little fortress. We were amazed at what we had built with our hands and our minds. No one could destroy it except God and his rain.

We were wet and hungry. A snake ran across the rocks. We climbed up the bank and ran to the open gate as fast as our tiny feet could go. I looked up to see a name over the gate. It surely says Heaven. I smell Mammie's homemade bread. I fasten the latch on the gate. We run to Mammie's arms. We're safe now. Oh how I loved her because she first loved me.

GRW

The Old Home Place

While living in my mom and dad's house your dad heard that Arnold and Pauline Render, my uncle and aunt, were selling their home place. Your dad loved working the land. He wanted a farm so bad. We went to the Bank and borrowed the money. We made big plans before moving. I ordered 50 baby chickens. I went to the Post Office to get them with you, Ronnie, and Brad with me. Mammie Igleheart watched Paddy. I made a place in the kitchen for the baby chicks.

I fixed your dad's lunch and food for us and we all went to our new home in the country. It was February and March and cold. We kept a fire burning in an old stove to keep warm. Your dad went to work and I painted and took care of the three of you until he picked us up a little after 11pm. We hired a Mr. Brown and Hoyt Kimmel to remodel the living room and bedrooms. They put down a hardwood floor and your dad sanded and varnished it. It looked so pretty. We moved in late March. After we moved I made curtains.

We were so happy to have our own place. The barn was nice too. Your dad loved breaking ground, with his horse and plow, for our big garden.

Year after year the place looked more and more like a farm. We all worked hard. We loved it.

I'm so thankful that all of you, our children, had the wonderful experience of a farm life and going to church in a small town, Centertown. I'm blessed to have such a loving family.

I love you,

Mama

GRW

Come Home to Bluegrass

song for Bill Monroe

(have the fiddler sound her call first)
When the whippoorwill calls it's time to go.
She's calling me home, home to Bluegrass.

The old saying goes, the old timer says,
it's time to plant corn when you hear her call.

Now she's calling me, telling me to come home,
come home, come home to Bluegrass.

I can hear her now, that lonesome lament.
She sings her song from the old gate post.

She's begging me and I must go. She's telling me
to come on home, come home to Bluegrass.

I'll roam the hills and plant my corn
and listen to the call of the whippoorwill.

She'll sit on the post of the garden gate
and together we'll sing Come Home to Bluegrass.

She'll sit on the post of the garden gate
and together we'll sing Come Home to Bluegrass.

(have the fiddler sound her call as you sing)
Come Home to Bluegrass
Come Home to Bluegrass

GRW

Mama's note: I remember listening to the whippoorwill and loving its call. I was lying in bed with the window open—it was on the gate post that opened going to the bee hives. The whippoorwill is nearly extinct. Its habitat has been destroyed. I haven't heard one since the 70's.

Look Up and Look Beyond

I see beyond horizons.
I study the clouds.

Look up and look beyond.

GRW

THE INTERVIEWS: Ron Interviews Mama

> ...*How they linger ever near me,*
> *and the sacred past unfolds.*
> *Precious memories, how they linger,*
> *how they ever flood my soul...*
> *In the stillness of the midnight,*
> *precious sacred scenes unfold.*

RON: This is Ron Whitehead. Today is Wednesday, July the 16th, 2014. I'm in Beaver Dam, Kentucky, visiting Mama. Mama and I are sitting at her kitchen table here looking at a banjo and a ukulele, and a lot of memorabilia, photos and recordings. I drove down from Louisville today. I took the backroad, the way we used to drive when we traveled from our farm outside of Centertown and drove up to visit Granddaddy and Mamaw in Valley View in Valley Station, Kentucky. We drove up through Hartford and Dundee and Fordsville and Hardinsburg and Irvington to Tiptop, down Dixie Highway, down Muldraugh Hill until we landed in Valley Station, which for the longest time I thought was Louisville, all of Louisville.

I'm here to interview—to do an oral tradition conversation—have a conversation with my mother, with Mama, for this—my new book and recording project, which is titled MAMA. The focus of this entire project is on my mother. And so let's get the ball rolling. Mama, will you please tell us—

MAMA: (singing) My dog has fleas...okay, Ron, let's go.

RON: Mama, please tell everybody your full name and your date of birth.

MAMA: I was born Greta Render. And I was born May 23, '32. And my mom, she loved the movie star Greta Garbo. So she named me after Greta Garbo, but she wanted to just say Greta because it didn't sound—she didn't want me to be exactly like—sound like Greta Garbo. So she named me Greta.

I was born in Matanzas to a handsome couple, a very talented musician and a writer. And, you know, my mom and dad could do anything.

And so what else do you want to know?

RON: You were born in Matanzas. Matanzas is outside of Centertown, towards the Green River. Centertown is a little community, population 323 now, but at one time it had up to 2,000 population.

And Matanzas is towards—what road is it on?

MAMA: That's—you go toward—out of Centertown, you go toward—it's called Big Rivers now, toward the Green River.

RON: Toward Green River, and Island and Livermore, McLean County. And the town is in Ohio County where bluegrass music was birthed, where the Monroe brothers grew up.

And Mama, you were born in Matanzas at what home? Were you born—

MAMA: It was in a little house close to my Grandmother Igleheart and my granddad. And Jo was born in the same house.

It was a little coal mining house. When the coal mines—some of the underground mines went out of business and a lot of people bought those little homes and they built onto them and fixed them up real nice.

Well, my mom—that's how talented she was. She could decorate a house of any kind in a matter of a couple days. And it looked like—it went from nothing to like somebody had been living there for years.

And anyway, we wanted to move out of that little place where we were by our grandparents. So back then it wasn't hard to move a little house. And my dad, well, he could figure out anything.

He got his friends and they put that little house on a type of lowboy and a tractor and pulled it up the road, probably two miles, at least, or three, and parked it in our grandparents'—Herman and Lola Bennett Render's—farm. Pappy gave Daddy part of his farm.

And it was close to the Montgomery brothers, they were always so talented, and Marjorie, their sister.

Well, that was in the afternoon. And Daddy and Momma fixed that little house up real quick, and it looked like a home already.

One night. Then the next morning the Montgomery brothers and Marjorie told us about this:

They went to the mailbox. They lived just a few feet from where we had moved this house to. And they said they looked up the lane and saw a house with kids out front and they said my goodness, when did that happen, what's going on here.

And I can see them now smiling from ear to ear and telling about Dick Render moving his family up the road a piece. And we lived there for years until we moved to Centertown.

RON: Well, and the Montgomery brothers, we will talk some more about them, they were special. When they smiled they all smiled together, they were all teeth.

MAMA: So wonderful to live by.

RON: Yeah, wonderful people, and incredible musicians and singers.

Okay. Now, tell us your parents' names.

MAMA: Momma was—her name was Louverine Igleheart, of course. And she met—I forget how she met Daddy. His name was Raymond Thomas Render.

Anyway, she was a cute little thing, and he was handsome. He was kind of Greek looking—I think that's where we come from, anyway—dark complected.

And they got married, she was 16, and went to Rockport, Indiana, and married, where a lot of people went back in those days, and made them a home at Matanzas by my—well, we didn't call that a home.

Our first home was really when we moved up there by the Montgomery brothers on Pappy's farm. That was our first real little home, because in Matanzas we were back and forth at our Grandparent Igleheart's house. And then—anyway.

RON: Was that the same house Mammie and Granddaddy Igleheart—was that the same house that I used to visit when I was a little boy way down—

MAMA: No, no, no. Un-un. No. See, that was—no. That was—Daddy Charlie built that house that you remember.

He was—oh, he could—he was an artist in a way. He was a carver. He carved out a lot of things, and he—they built that little house, that's the one you remember, and had the stone front, like a fence around the front yard, and the gate. You remember the gate.

RON: It was beautiful.

MAMA: It was a cute little house. And he had a little barn, and he had one cow, and he had bees.

Oh, gosh. I remember him taking the honey out. And they were so—well, like most people back then, they had to save. Mammie was—she taught me to save.

She would—I would be at her house a lot. She had a little old sweet little kitchen and an iron stove. And I remember—one time I remember best of all where I learned how to save.

She would pour me half a cup of milk. Not like they do today, run things over. And she said if you want more, I will give it to you.

And so that's where I learned how to save and be thrifty like she was.

And I remember Daddy Charlie—a lot of people had to leave. They would go north. And Daddy Charlie, he went to work at the Ford plant in Michigan.

And he got to talk to Henry Ford. He learned to like Henry. Well, Daddy Charlie come home. He had another job to do back home.

He come home and he carved a cute little Model T out of wood and he sent that to Henry Ford. And Henry sent him a letter back saying how he loved it and what a good wood carver he was and how talented he was.

RON: Did he put that in a jug? Is that the Model T that you—

MAMA: I don't know if it was a jug, or it might have just been—

RON: Just out.

MAMA: Yeah. I don't know but he put a lot of carvings in jugs. That was amazing. People didn't believe anybody could do that.

He would go see something, just look at it. Like he went to—down the road where they were building a bridge and he saw this concrete mixer, the old-timey concrete mixer. And he went back home and he started working on the concrete mixer in a big jug. He put that together just like the real thing.

And I remember I got one of his bottles. Someone gave that to me. They called me and said I know you would love to have this bottle.

It's an airplane and it's got 1932 on the wings. And that's when I was born. And it was amazing that he did that.

I was so thrilled to get that bottle with that airplane in it with the date of my birth and—

RON: That he carved.

MAMA: Yeah, he carved it and put it piece by piece into the bottle. It was amazing how he could put his carved wood pieces through a little tiny neck bottle.

RON: I saw some of his animals and machines and automobiles in jugs.

MAMA: Yeah. I still have a few.

RON: He made a rattlesnake rattler belt.

MAMA: And corn presses.

RON: He killed so many rattlesnakes where they lived.

MAMA: And my Mammie, she was so talented as a self-taught seamstress. She would sew dresses and quilts and everything by using her little old fingers.

RON: Did you learn to quilt from Mammie Igleheart?

MAMA: Yeah, she had the big old-timey quilt frames that you had to set up in your bedroom, living room, wherever there was room. And I would go see her. I would stay for days at their house.

And she had a little toy iron stove, similar to what she cooked on in the kitchen, but it was a toy. And I would get under Mammie's quilting frame and act like I would cook. It had little bitty—little bitty iron skillets and pans.

And I would be a cookin. And I would reach up with a spoon, and she would take that spoon and put it in her mouth and act like she was eating with me. And she was such a joy to be around and an entertainer. Us kids—we all loved her.

RON: I did, too.

MAMA: It was a good life down there.

RON: Let me ask you this. You're journeying back here to earlier memories, is there a particular memory that stands out as your first memory, or one of your first memories?

MAMA: Oh, heck yeah. I remember way back. Let me see.

There was one where I was two years old.

Oh, we were—Momma and my Mammie Igleheart, her mom, were picking blackberries down there by their house. And Mammie and Pappy—Daddy Charlie, I called him—had a dog.

And I was—we were on a high bank, a pretty little branch. The water flowed down it. And Momma put us on a little quilt, Jo and me. I was two.

They were picking blackberries, and I went around this tree to—it was leaning over the branch. I was always daring, even at two years old.

Well, the dog tried to get in between me and the tree, and I fell in the branch.

That's one thing I remember when I was two, but anyway.

RON: You were always daring?

MAMA: Yes. I still am. I still got my biker's license.

RON: Your biker's license.

MAMA: But I got sense enough not to go buy a bike. I better not get on a motorcycle.

RON: Do you ever want to get on one?

MAMA: Yeah, I do.

RON: Okay. Now, how—you're the oldest of 13. So you were the first born.

MAMA: Yes.

RON: And I'm your first born of six.

Now, how much younger is the next in line, Jo Carolyn, who is going to join us and sing some songs in a few minutes?

MAMA: Well, I will tell you what, we're almost twins.

RON: Almost twins?

MAMA: Everybody thinks we are twins. She is 17 months younger.

RON: There's a little breathing room there.

MAMA: But we started singing when we were very young. I was a born alto. And I can remember Momma standing me up on the little kitchen table—and speaking of kitchen, Daddy had that—that house we moved was just two rooms. And Daddy added that little kitchen on there in a couple of days and of course Momma had it all fixed up in no time.

RON: So he just added an entire kitchen on in two days?

MAMA: Yeah. We lived in a two-room house with a kitchen.

Anyway, Momma, she stood me up on the kitchen table and dressed me in a cute little old dress. And you had the cute high top lace up shoes back then and pretty little socks. And I can remember her doing that.

And I was probably—well, I was going on four. I know I was, because we were getting ready to go to Calhoun.

Daddy had met this fiddler, Stanley Hicks. He was such a great fiddle player. Even I thought back then, when I was so little, that he was wonderful. And then later on I heard different people talk about him and how good he was.

So Momma and Daddy took me and Jo to Calhoun to Stanley's home. I remember his mom. She was a real sweet woman.

And Daddy and him—he and Daddy played music there, but, you know, I don't remember singing and I know we did.

RON: You and Jo started singing when you were—

MAMA: Four and five.

RON: —four and five.

MAMA: Yeah. I'd sing alto and Jo soprano, and we'd just sing it.

RON: So you were natural soprano and alto?

MAMA: One of our songs, first one, was Whispering Hope. We will sing it after a while, but—

RON: So Granddaddy was already singing and performing?

MAMA: Oh, yeah, he was—before they married he recorded somewhere in Indiana. He did recordings.

RON: Richmond, Indiana?

MAMA: I forgot.

RON: That's one of the earlier places. Akron, Ohio, and Richmond, Indiana were two of the earliest places where country music and jazz were recorded.

A lot of people don't know that. So you recorded—I knew he recorded in Akron, did a lot of recording there. I didn't know about Richmond.

MAMA: He was young when they—when they first went—a lot of people went up there just like they did to Michigan.

My family—Daddy's family went to Akron because his two brothers were already there and a sister. And his brothers were barbers, and that's where Daddy learned to barber. He never went to school. I don't think any of them did, but he was a wonderful barber.

Anyway, he—that's when he started doing—play parties and singing on the radio at—it was West Virginia. I forgot the name of the radio station.

RON: It's historically one of the—Wheeling, West Virginia.

MAMA: Wheeling, yeah. It was Wheeling.

RON: The most power goes out all over that part of the country to several states.

MAMA: That's where it was, because I got a postcard especially made for him—they did in Wheeling. It's got his picture and name and number where you could call and hire him for parties or whatever.

RON: All the country stars sang on that—performed on that station.

MAMA: So then he—when he came home—it was when Momma and Daddy met, there were always play parties.

RON: That's what they were called, play parties.

MAMA: Oh, yeah. I remember one, it was at Matanzas when we—after we had moved up toward Walton's Creek. We would come back to Matanzas to our friends' homes, and they would roll back the carpet.

They had old-timey carpets. We would roll them up and bring everybody into the living room with the band and they would have music and dance, whatever you wanted to do.

RON: So when did you start dancing?

MAMA: Oh, well, I just—

RON: When you could walk?

MAMA: Yeah. Yeah. I loved dancing. I love square dancing, any kind.

RON: Any kind of dancing?

MAMA: Waltz.

RON: So when did you play—what was first the first instrument you learned to play? Spoons, washboard? Was it a—

MAMA: Oh, well, it was spoons and washboard. And when Daddy got a ukulele, I loved that little old ukulele, and I learned to play it, but—thinking about the washboard and the spoons, we were—Jo and I were on stage all of our lives, seemed like. And in school they would always ask us to join them in some kind of musical program.

And I forgot what Jo played but I played the best board and spoons. And I used thimbles for the washboard.

RON: Thimbles.

MOMMA: Thimbles, you put on the tips of your fingers. I got really good with that.

Anyway, everybody loved it, used to cheer and scream and holler. And of course we had all kinds of talented people at Centertown School, and we were in plays.

Anyway, Jo and I had been in the—they had—Hartford had—Ohio County had The Fort Hartford Story and we were in that. We sung some old songs and that was a wonderful program that we were in.

And even your dad was in it. He did something. Oh, we were in different dances. Your dad and I were Spanish people. And they did all kinds of dances in the—you know, like long time ago when there were—Hartford was called—it was Fort Hartford, I believe, Spaniards come through.

And the stories about Spaniards in this—places down on Rough River, and even Livermore where they found the Spaniards had camped out and even lived.

And so they had that Spanish music at that time in the Fort Hartford story that you and—me and your dad danced with the music.

RON: I think, what I read, there was a Spanish fort before it became another fort. So the Spaniards have been around for a long time in this area.

MAMA: So anyway, it's been an interesting life I have lived, I tell you.

One time a bunch from Nashville come up, and Daddy heard they were going to be in Hartford in the courthouse playing, playing music.

Well, we went to that. And we sat in there and listened to them, but when they got ready to leave, Daddy asked them—they were on their way to Fordsville School. They were going to do another program at Fordsville School.

And our dad, he didn't care. He would just go right up to people and talk to them. He said I would love to have my girls to sing with you all in your band when you go to Fordsville. Well, he talked to them a while and they said okay.

So I remember going to Fordsville and singing at the Fordsville School with Jo Carolyn. And the band—let's see, what was their names—like Blue Brass Fields Band was one that come to Hartford.

Anyway, one of the songs we sung is Whispering Hope and something else, but they just let us sing about three. And they gave us a few dollars. And, of course, we thought that was wonderful. We thought we were going to go on the road, I guess.

RON: How old were you?

MAMA: We were teenagers.

RON: Early teens?

MAMA: Twelve and thirteen, yeah. But Daddy tried his darndest to get us on the—to go on the road, which I'm glad he didn't. We were—when we became older teenagers we kind of backed down.

We don't—we didn't want much to do with the life like that, ever since we started singing.

People would call on us to sing at funerals and weddings. And that's about what we have done all of our life, is—of course, we would sing at World War II programs. We did a lot of those, sing When Johnny Comes Marching Home and White Cliffs of Dover.

And one time in church we got a program of—the music teacher, she didn't—wasn't too hot on doing programs. So Jo and I, we asked her if we could do one for the Fourth of July.

Well, we got different ones in Centertown to do things in the musical. And that went over so good. Everybody loved it. It was—we had people to march in like World War II soldiers. We had a sailor and a Marine dressed up in the real uniforms and different ones—little ones carried the flags. And it was a beautiful program.

And even now we talk of doing some at McHenry. We haven't done one yet at our church where we go. We love to—you know, when we do that, we love to do it big. And we put on concerts before, because all of our family is talented. And I recorded some of those.

Once we was helping out a little boy in Centertown. He was real sick, had some kind of disease. So we asked somebody in the PTA if we could put on a program, a benefit program for that little thing. He was so sweet.

And so we got all of our families together on stage. Of course, we practiced a little bit. We don't like to practice. I don't. I just like to get up there and do my thing.

RON: I'm the same way.

MAMA: Yeah. Jo Carolyn had her family singing. I had my family singing. And because of our initials, WP, and the old WPA—our dad was in charge of the WPA. Workmen's progress, whatever. It was back in the '40s.

RON: Yeah.

MAMA: So we called that the WPA Association Gang. That went over big and we made a pretty good amount of money for that little boy and his family. That was one concert we did.

RON: Let me ask you this, since we're on music. You mentioned before that you all a time or two went up to Rosine to Jerusalem Ridge and sat on the front porch and sang with the Monroe boys, performed with them back in the day.

MAMA: Well, I will tell you about this.

Yeah, Mom and Daddy, me and Jo went up—it was a steep hill. We were going to the Monroe house that's still there.

And there's two ways to go in. We went in the one that's a steep hill. Of course, it wasn't very good back then, and it was—had a little gravel on it.

Well, Daddy's old car quit and we started going back down the hill. Momma was screaming her head off, Raymond, Raymond, what are you going to do?!

And, of course, Daddy, he stopped it. He wasn't scared of anything.

We got down to the bottom of the hill and we tried it again and made it, but I don't remember singing up there. I know we did, but it wasn't Bill Monroe. It was his brother.

RON: Charlie?

MAMA: Yeah, Charlie, but I remember walking across that porch. I loved that porch, and I just remember the house.

RON: It's a pretty house.

MAMA: Oh, yeah, and I loved it.

Well, Daddy had his guitar. So he and Charlie would play and sing. And we probably sung a song, but we were just amazed at the home and being up there. It was so pretty in the woods.

RON: Yeah, yeah. Okay. One more thing about the music.

The Everly Brothers, Mose Rager, Ike and his sons Phil and Don who became known as The Everly Brothers.

Now, Mose, he is a legendary figure in the roots of country music, and he had a barber shop over in—

MAMA: Drakesboro. It was in Drakesboro.

RON: And you all would go over there. And I understand that Mose came over to Granddaddy's barber shop in Centertown, as well, and they performed together.

MAMA: See, Daddy got—Daddy loved music. Of course, he was into recording. He knew all about recordings.

And so he bought him a recorder that made records. And it would cut—you know, you could sing on it.

RON: I remember when I was a little boy singing in one of those.

MAMA: It would cut a record.

RON: Yeah.

MAMA: So one day we went to Mose Rager's barber shop in Drakesboro. And, of course, being both barbers, they had a lot in common. And Mose was—he was a musician.

Well, they played together. And I don't know what songs that we sung. I don't have any idea, but I know that—remember being there, and they were such nice people.

RON: Do you remember The Everly—the boys singing at all?

MAMA: No, I don't, but I went to their concert. My mom said we were related way down the road, you know what they call it.

RON: Through the Iglehearts.

MAMA: The Jameses, Iglehearts—

RON: The Iglehearts, the graveyard is in Muhlenberg County.

MAMA: Anyway, some relation, but Daddy really loved them. They could really harmonize, like Jo and I would harmonize.

RON: Yeah.

MAMA: But I have been to their concerts, and I don't—

RON: I loved going to that one with you in Central City, The Everly Brothers and John Prine.

MAMA: Yeah, that was good.

RON: Now, let me ask you: Earlier you mentioned your move from—family move from Matanzas to Walton's Creek.

Now, Walton's Creek, that's where once upon a time there was a one room school.

Was that the first school you attended?

MAMA: That was the first school I attended, yes.

RON: How old were you, five? Were you five?

MAMA: Well, I think, yeah, I was five. And Jo cried because she wanted to go with me because we were so close but I went ahead to school there.

And I had the best teachers, Ms. Wilma Kirtley, married a Williams, and Hazel Elmore Peters. Oh, Ms. Hazel, she was such a sweet lady. I have got a picture of her that's going to be in the book.

And anyway, on the way to school one day it was rainy and muddy and cold, I fell in the mud.

And I remember, too—go back a little bit. The Montgomery brothers would always walk to school with us. They would walk behind us, all three of them, talking and smiling.

And Ms. Wilma and Ms. Hazel put me by the old timey stove and put the—shielded me with some kind of curtain, probably, and took my dress off and washed it and dried it and put it back on me right there in the school.

I remember so many things about the Walton's Creek School. They had pie suppers and big Christmas programs. And Anthony, he lived close to the school. He had a big bushy beard and he played Santa Claus.

Well, I thought sure that was Santa Claus knocking on the door, that big Christmas program they had. And I was in some kind of Christmas program that year. Momma had me in a little red dress. And the teacher stood me up on a stool, and I sang--Up on the Housetop—about reindeers being on the housetop and—Old St. Nick.

Yeah, yeah, I sang that song by myself. I think back, and I couldn't believe it, because I was so bashful, but I stood up on that stool and sang that cute little song. I think it's three verses.

RON: Now, let me ask you this: Walton's Creek Church is just across from where that one room school was, and the graveyard is there. And that's where a lot of the Renders are buried, including—

MAMA: Bennett, Civil War soldier. My—my great grandfather, Jacob Bennett, married Frances Jagoe. She was a little dark complected, cute little woman. Of course, that's where my Mammie Render comes from. That's her mom and dad.

And the Jagoes—there are several Jagoes in Owensboro. Just recently we all got together, the sisters and I went to see one of the Jagoe boys and his family.

They were so nice. They took us right in, and they had pictures of our distant relatives, the Jagoe people, dark complected and beautiful. And that was such an amazing trip to meet the Jagoe family that we had never met before.

RON: Granddaddy and Mamaw are buried there, and you had two siblings who died when they were real little. Can you say something about them and what you remember of them?

MAMA: I remember Eddie Bennett Render being born. And he was a little sick, sickly baby, little sickly boy. He was so cute, but he had the blood disease that a lot of little babies died of.

And Mammie Render came over and washed the little body and made a little white gown-like outfit and put it on him. And that was—yeah. I would watch her.

RON: How long did he live?

MAMA: I always wanted to watch things. I wasn't scared of anything.

Oh, he was just three months old.

Then my little sister was born in Centertown. We lived there behind the barber shop. Suzanne. She was born before you were born.

Of course, I was married. I was pregnant with you. And her name was Suzanne. She was still born.

And I was with Momma while she was having that little baby with me being pregnant. Of course, that didn't bother me. And our next door neighbor Roberta Watkins, she would come over, such a sweet neighbor, and she helped Dr. Allen and Momma give birth to that little girl.

And I remember burying her at Walton's Creek beside my little brother. And it was so sad to me. I couldn't quit crying, and—I don't know. I don't think it had anything to do with—

RON: You were pregnant with me?

MAMA: I don't think you were (inaudible).

RON: Maybe that's why I've experienced so much melancholy in my life.

MAMA: Could be. But anyway, I couldn't quit crying because thinking about—she was so pretty.

RON: It's interesting to...

MAMA: She was born in the '50s, like you.

RON: Well, I have always—nobody has ever talked about that, and I have always been curious about those two babies.

MAMA: Well, my Lord.

RON: That's the first time I have heard anything about it.

MAMA: I would have told you all about it. When we get together, there's so many of us. Even now we forget to tell you about—I try to tell you everything that's happening down here. But didn't really want to relay messages over the phone, whatever, Facebook now.

RON: Well, now, being the oldest of 13, you had to be like a second mother to your brothers and sisters.

MAMA: Oh, well, yeah, but that didn't bother me. I just jumped in and did things.

And we used to—we lived by the Montgomery brothers in that house, I would wash cloth diapers, and Momma would—I would wash the diapers and whatever on the washboard.

And Jo and I would put the quilts in a big old metal tub. Called it a washtub. I remember us washing—I had a quilt out and we would get in there with our bare feet and stomp around.

Momma was clean as a pin. The quilt wasn't that dirty but she had to have everything clean.

Well, we finally got it in another tub to rinse it. And we rinsed it—we took it out of the water. Jo got on one end of the quilt and I was on the other and we went in opposite directions to twist it and wring the water out.

It was so heavy. We finally got it on the line to dry, but we—yeah.

RON: So you started learning about how to take care of a house and take care of kids when you were still a kid?

MAMA: Well, it just came natural, so—I just did it.

RON: So you all moved from Matanzas to Walton's Creek. Then where after that? To Centertown, or someplace—

MAMA: To Centertown, yeah. That was a big move, because see—well, Daddy, sometimes he would have to walk from Walton's Creek home or catch a ride, but most of the time he had a car, an old Model T, and to barber.

And he had a cute little old barber shop out there by a little old Centertown restaurant. It was Bishop's Cafe. And that's where I learned to shine shoes. I mean, I picked that up in a jiffy. I could use those brushes and pop that rag.

RON: You taught me how to do that.

MAMA: And we made a—it was probably ten cents a shine. And sometime Jo would do it, too, and make a few cents.

But anyway, we moved to Centertown. And—oh, Lord. Well, the house—this—we moved so many times, so many places, but I will tell you about this house.

Daddy found out the Olaton School, it wasn't going to be anymore. It was a nice building. It was full of windows.

And so he found out that he could—he could buy it and...

(end of tape one; beginning of tape two)

RON: We're going to get back to the Olaton story. You all go ahead and pick out—go ahead and do the songs. We're going to get back to Mama telling all the different places she lived in her first 18 years before she started her own family, but right now, my Aunt Jo Carolyn happened to walk in the door.

And Mama has been talking about her little sister. A lot of people thought they were twins. I think Mama said 17 months difference in their age. Jo is the next in line in the pecking order of 13 children.

Mama and Jo have performed thousands of times. And Jo was born a soprano and Mama was born an alto.

They're going to share a few songs with us now sitting here at the kitchen table in Beaver Dam, Kentucky.

MAMA: Okay, Jo, this is The River of Memory.

JO CAROLYN: This is about the old childhood...It could be us, too.

Song: Did you ever go sailing down the river of memory to the home of the—

JO CAROLYN: I changed the words.

Song: Did you ever go sailing down the river of memory to the home of your childhood that is nestled by the old maple tree. Where the sunshine is cheery, and nothing in the world is dreary. It's the home of your childhood down the river of memory.

MAMA: Okay, Jo. Now, one of the first songs we sang— I spoke earlier on the tape about our first song we ever sung.

JO CAROLYN: It was In the Garden.

MAMA: Let's sing a little bit of In the Garden.

Song: I come to the garden alone when the dew is still on the roses. And the voice I hear falling on my ear, the Son of God discloses. And He walks with me, and He talks with me, and He tells me I am his own. And the joy we share as we tarry there none other has ever known.

JO CAROLYN: I'm Jo Carolyn, and I remember the words of all these songs, but I have to depend on Greta for other things. She remembers everything.

MAMA: Well, I can't—I about lost my memory on a lot of things.

Okay. You got Whippoorwill? You got Whippoorwill, or what do you want to sing next? One of our old songs. Just one.

Song: There's a whippoorwill sweetly singing in the pale moon light. Whippoorwill, whippoorwill. And he is singing a song that makes me long for home tonight. Whippoorwill, whippoorwill. He sings about the honeysuckle around the cabin door. Seems he is saying someone is praying you will come back once more. There's a whippoorwill sweetly singing in the pale moon light. Now I know, I must go, whippoorwill.

MAMA: We sang that at our precious sister Linda's funeral. And we talked about her being in heaven and how she would be talking to everybody up there and listening to the whippoorwill. And that was one of the songs we sang at her funeral.

You want to sing that one, Jo?

JO CAROLYN: That's a good one.

RON: I grew up listening to that song too.

MAMA: Oh, yeah, I know you did.

Song: In a vine covered shack in the mountain bravely fighting the battle of time, there's a dear one who's weathered life's sorrow, it's that silver haired Daddy of mine. If I could recall all the heartaches dear old Daddy I've caused you to bear. If I could erase the lines from your face and bring back the gold to your hair. If God would but grant me the power to turn back the pages of time, I would give all I own, if I could but atone to that silver haired Daddy of mine.

MAMA: Oh, that was always a good one, a favorite.

What do we want to sing next? What do you have?

Oh, The Old Pine Tree was everybody's favorite. Yeah, my grandson Atticus, he loves that. He sings it, plays it on the guitar. I think all the kids love this song.

The old ones are coming back.

RON: This song haunted me. I sang it to myself up in that attic I slept in for years.

MAMA: Did you really?

RON: Yeah. The wind would be whistling through the holes in the wall, coming through the cedar and the pine tree. And this song, I couldn't get it out of my head. I love this song.

JO CAROLYN: When we sing it now at get-togethers, my kids get tears in their eyes. And Greta did a while ago when we were over here and we was practicing.

Daddy is where we got a lot of our songs, from Daddy, the things that he used to sing. And, of course, his songs were the blues.

MAMA: Yeah, he could sing the blues.

Song: When they cut down the old pine tree and they hauled it away to the mill...Hauled it away to the mill to make a coffin of pine for the sweetheart of mine when they cut down the old pine tree. Stop a while and listen to my story. I just come down from the hill. I went there to find my childhood sweetheart with the roses and the whippoorwills. I went there to look for the old pine tree where we carved our hearts long ago, but the old pine tree was gone, and my love for her lingers on. Oh, they cut down the old pine tree and they hauled it away to the mill to make a coffin of pine for that sweetheart of mine when they cut down the old pine tree.

MAMA: That brings back memories. You want to sing another one, Jo?

JO CAROLYN: Well, I think you wanted this old religious song, didn't you, Ronnie?

RON: I did.

MAMA: Let's do it.

JO CAROLYN: Where is it?

MAMA: Here is one we used to sing—sometime we would go to rest homes. And there was an old rest home in Hartford we would go to. And the old people would love this song, When You and I Were Young Maggie. Let's see if we can get that.

Song: I wandered today to the hill, Maggie, to watch the stream below. The creek and the old creaking mill, Maggie, as we used to long long time ago. The green road is gone from the hill, Maggie, when first the daisies sprung The creaking old mill is still, Maggie, since you and I were young.

MAMA: We must've messed up, because—

JO CAROLYN: Our eyes are getting bad. We can't see those little words.

MAMA: We hadn't sung that in forever. Pick out another one. You got a mark here. I'll Fly Away. Ronnie, you join us.

RON: This is one of my favorite songs.

Song: Some bright morning when this life is o'er, I'll fly away to a home on God's celestial shore, I'll fly away. I'll fly away, old glory, I'll fly away. When I die hallelujah by and by, I'll fly away.

JO CAROLYN: Amen.

MAMA: That's a good one. Oh, golly. Yeah, all my kids love that one.

RON: Have you got one more in you?

MAMA: Whispering Hope was one of the old ones we used to sing. We will sing a little bit of that one. That's it.

Song: Soft as a voice of an angel breathing a lesson unheard. Hope with a gentle persuasion whispers her comforting word. Wait till the darkness is over. Wait till the tempest is done. Hope for the sunshine tomorrow after the shower is gone. Whispering hope, whispering hope, welcome back home making my heart in its sorrow rejoice.

RON: Before you stop, you sang during and after the war. You were going to sing a couple of war songs.

MAMA: I'm getting hoarse. All right.

When we lived in Louisville during the war, I remember the blackouts we had. We were warned, whenever the siren—loud siren came on, we had to pull the shades and draw the curtains and no lights whatsoever.

That happened several times when we lived there on Algonquin Parkway, close to Algonquin Park.

And so we thought of the boys when they went overseas. And some of them didn't get to come back home, and it was a very sad time, but we remember a lot about things during the war.

And that's when we went from Louisville to Jeffersonville. Dad worked at the shipyards and went over to Elizabeth, Indiana. He barbered there and drove back and forth to the shipyards.

Then we all got homesick, especially Daddy. He wanted to come home. So we got in the car, just like gypsies, and come home to Centertown.

Everywhere Daddy went Momma wanted to go. They were so much in love. And so it didn't matter where Daddy went, Momma would go. And, of course, we would go too and we loved it. That was our life.

But here is one of the songs that we thought of when we thought about the war and living in Louisville. Okay, see if we can sing that.

Song: When the lights go on again all over the world, and the boys are home again all over the—

MAMA: Go ahead and sing it. I can't get it. Sing it.

Song: When the boys are home again all over the world, and rain or snow is all that will come from above, angel hearts will sing when the lights go on again all over the world.

RON: Good job.

JO CAROLYN: And I remember, we just had a radio, and we listened to the news every night. It was about the war every night.

And Daddy was over the radio guarding it. We couldn't talk. If we mentioned anything, he hit us. He said shut up. But the first boy that got killed from Ohio County was Welborn Lee Ashby. He died at Hawaii.

RON: Pearl Harbor.

JO CAROLYN: Pearl Harbor. And he was the first one, and they lived down the street from us. And it was so sad. It was so sad.

And we—there was another one that lived down the road from us when we lived at Walton's Creek, and they had one son, a big fine healthy son. He was in the Army. And they got word that the son had got killed, Charles Johnson.

MAMA: Oh, yeah.

JO CAROLYN: And he was such a big—Daddy would drive his old—whatever, about a 30-something vehicle, old square one. It might have been (inaudible).

And he would go to town with us, and Daddy would—instead of stopping, Daddy would say come on, get on, and he would run and jump on the fender and grab the glass.

Well, when he grabbed the glass one day it broke and cut a big gash out of his arm. I remember it. And he got killed in the Army, too.

MAMA: Yeah, I remember when they brought him home. It was so sad. It was awful.

JO CAROLYN: We will sing this one, and we will cut it off.

RON: Okay.

Song: There will be bluebirds over the white cliffs of Dover tomorrow, just you wait and see. There will be love and laughter, and peace ever after, tomorrow when the world is free. The shepherd will tend his sheep, the valley will bloom again, and Johnny will go to sleep in his own little room again. There will be bluebirds over the white cliffs of Dover tomorrow, just you wait and see.

RON: Beautiful. Thank you.

MAMA: We're out of breath.

RON: Thank you, Jo.

JO CAROLYN: You're welcome, Ronnie.

RON: Thank you for stopping by.

JO CAROLYN: And, Ronnie, I love you. I always have since you were born. It was a good life, us growing up. It was wonderful. I think you—it really helps you when you're growing up to go through a war. It makes you realize how blessed we are, our country. And war just does something to you. Now, when the war was over, I was 12.

MAMA: Yeah.

JO CAROLYN: And the bells were ringing everywhere. Well, Bill House had a big old cattle truck. And every kid and adult got in that old cattle truck, and we started driving. We made the whole loop, Rockport, Beaver Dam, all the way around and come back screaming and hollering, because the war was over. It was the most wonderful time.

MAMA: People would pick up anything they could get ahold of to bang on. I remember Daddy picked up the dinner bell and hit it and it cracked. It broke in two and it was just laying there in the yard. It cracked. He had to get something else.

JO CAROLYN: He was so excited, he rung it and broke it in two, but it was a good time.

RON: All right. Thank you Jo.

JO CAROLYN: You're welcome, Ronnie.

RON: Okay. Beautiful singing I grew up with, Mama and my Aunt Jo Carolyn, Mama's little sister.

So let's get Mama—folks, we're here at the kitchen table, Mama's kitchen table in Beaver Dam, Kentucky. Mama's home. I drove down today to visit with Mama and do this recording about her life, the first 18 years of it.

So, Mama, before you and Jo sang you started to tell the story about—you and your family had just moved to Centertown, and you were telling about Granddaddy, your dad, going up to Olaton. So let's pick that up where we left off.

MAMA: Okay. All right. We found out about the Olaton School wasn't going to be anymore, but the building was still good. I mean, it really looked good.

Jo and I went with Daddy and two of Daddy's friends to start tearing it down. And it was full of windows, nice windows, which we used in our—the house they were fixing to build.

Anyway, we loaded up. We made several trips, I'm sure, but I remember one trip we was with Daddy, we loaded that old truck up with windows and whatever.

And we were crossing the Olaton bridge. It was an old iron bridge and one wheel broke through the wood. They had a jack so they jacked that old truck up. And we went on, drove over it just fine, but we stopped at the Olaton Grocery Store. It's gone now, but—

RON: Olaton, that's a good distance from Centertown. That's in northern Ohio County. Ohio County is the fifth largest county in Kentucky.

MAMA: My daughter Paddy used to live there. It was – but it was a hilly—it was a beautiful little town.

RON: Fifteen miles from Centertown.

MAMA: Daddy said let's get something to eat at the store, a company store full of everything.

So Daddy sent Jo and me in. We got us a good old bologna sandwich. Nothing any better back then. They sliced it their self with an old butcher knife and put it on the crackers.

You know, crackers back then come in the one big piece, like four little pieces in one, but you can't find those anymore to put a big slab of bologna on.

RON: Put mustard on it.

MAMA: Yeah, of course. Now I use relish and hot sauce, whatever.

But anyway, Daddy started putting our house together. And he had Spadge Tooley, he had him on top of the house putting—we had the rafters up, and Daddy said that don't look right.

Well Spadge went up there on the ladder, he took an axe. He evened that rafter out, the eaves, with a chopping axe, and it worked just perfect.

RON: I swear. I swear.

MAMA: But Daddy, he knew how to do things, he and Mom together. We had hardwood floors in that house. Of course, we always kept them waxed and shiny.

And we had the little front entrance like people had in the '40s, in the late '40s, yeah.

Anyway, the next move—well, golly, I can get my years mixed up, but the next move, we went to Vine Grove, because he was called to—he was a good grader man. He was so good, he could just level off a bank to the T exactly the way the contractor wanted it.

RON: And a grader—for our listeners, some won't know—a grader is heavy equipment with that long blade.

MAMA: Yeah. Hard to do, but he didn't—nobody had to tell him. He did it—got it down to the very T, like I said.

And he was called to work at—build Muldraugh Hill around Fort Knox.

RON: At Fort Knox between—okay, Vine Grove is outside of E-Town, and it's near Tiptop, and it's near Fort Knox.

MAMA: That's where he worked, Tiptop.

RON: That's where you all lived and he worked at Tiptop, on Dixie Highway.

MAMA: Yeah. Everywhere we went we camped out, more or less.

RON: Gypsies.

MAMA: Oh yeah. We loved it. I still do. I could live right now in a treehouse but getting back to Vine Grove, Daddy barbered there. Everywhere he went he barbered because he loved it.

Had a little barber shop there. Then he would work I guess late afternoon, barber shop, and go work—you know, he was a tough guy.

RON: So he was a tough guy.

MAMA: Yeah.

RON: But barbering was quick cash, plus it was storytelling, too. People exchanged stories.

MAMA: He told stories. He coon hunted and did everything else while he was cutting somebody's hair. I'm surprised that they come out looking good, but they always did.

But anyway, the next move—well, I skipped Fordsville. That's back before Vine Grove. Then we lived on Western Kentucky University campus.

RON: In Bowling Green.

MAMA: He barbered there beside a restaurant, yeah, and we lived upstairs over the restaurant. That was an exciting trip. That was right after the flood.

RON: 1937 flood.

MAMA: I missed that story.

That was before Vine Grove. Daddy—we were at our Pappy Render's house while they were moving into the Bowling Green area, and during that time the flood happened. I remember the '37 flood. I was five.

RON: You were five years old, yeah.

MAMA: So Daddy come somehow to get us, because I remember riding in a boat. I don't know whereabouts it was, but he was taking us to Bowling Green. I remember the '37 flood. Okay. Back to...

RON: Wait a minute. Wait a minute. Well, where was— so where were you all living in '37 during the big flood, in Fordsville or Centertown? Do you remember?

MAMA: No. See, time—

RON: Is that when you moved to Bowling Green?

MAMA: We moved so fast that's why it's hard for me to tell it.

RON: Would you live in the back of the car sometimes?

MAMA: Oh, at Vine Grove, yeah.

Okay, the next move was to—let me think—Louisville during—Lord, I'm skipping a lot here, but anyway, we went to Louisville. We lived in the chicken house there, and it was a nice one.

RON: A nice chicken house?

MAMA: Yeah. Evidently somebody had just moved out of it.

RON: Was that during World War II?

MAMA: Yeah. It was beside my aunt and uncle, Ruth and Paul Mabrey.

RON: Algonquin Parkway.

MAMA: Yeah, yeah. That's when the lights went out during the war, and we had to—you know. Anyway.

All right the next trip, Daddy was called to—he barbered there too. Daddy was called to the shipyards in Jeffersonville and I'm sure that he built—

RON: During World War II.

MAMA: —helped build LST and different little old boats, but that was a big deal there.

And he would—during lunch somebody would come around he got acquainted with, he said they would say Dick, I need a haircut. Well, he would stop eating and go cut that man's hair.

RON: So he took his barber equipment with him to work at Jeff Boat?

MAMA: Everywhere, yeah.

RON: So I wonder what kind of work he did there, welding or—

MAMA: I don't know. One day we were there waiting for him to get off work and the big horn went off. Somebody got hurt. And word got to us that somebody got killed.

Lord, Momma lost it, but, you know, it wasn't Daddy. It was a sad thing, but it wasn't Daddy.

So after us hanging around and living in an apartment in Jeffersonville, we moved across the river to Elizabeth, Indiana.

RON: Okay. You moved up the river. Jeffersonville was—

MAMA: Up, over, or wherever.

RON: Well, it's just across from Louisville on the Indiana side.

Elizabeth is just on down the road from Clarksville. I live in historic Clarksville with Jinn now. So that's not far from—she took me up to Elizabeth.

MAMA: It's a beautiful little town.

RON: It's still a pretty little place. We looked for a barber shop up there but I guess it's long gone.

MAMA: I don't have any idea, but anyway, he barbered there, too, of course.

We had a cute little house. I think I mentioned it in the book, but Daddy raised a huge garden. It was so pretty.

And Momma—I would take Momma—Momma couldn't drive, but I will go back to Centertown about my driver's license.

See, Momma couldn't drive then when we were young. And I was 13, and Daddy was busy in the shop and doing grading work on the side, and he needed somebody to take Momma shopping or wherever.

So he took me to the courthouse. I'm pretty sure it was Mr. Blankenship. Daddy talked to him. Daddy knew everybody. He said this girl needs her driver's license.

And so he just wrote me out a driver's license. I didn't take no test or anything. And I have been driving since I was 13. And I was good, because I just jumped in that old—you know, different vehicles and drove and—where am I in the story?

RON: Here or there, which is fine. I like this. This is fine. This is okay, because we're staying within the first 18 years of your life. So wherever we go, it doesn't have to be in chronological order.

MAMA: No, it's really funny and exciting. We have lived a good life and colorful.

RON: Yeah, I would say.

MAMA: One time at the restaurant in Beaver Dam they know about you and how colorful you are, Ron, and me. And I go in all, you know, different colors, and I'm friendly and I speak to everybody. Everybody loves me. I'm bragging, but everybody loves me.

And one guy said Ron is just real colorful, just like you, his mother. And so—

RON: Somebody said that to you?

MAMA: Yeah.

RON: Isn't that the truth.

MAMA: Where am I?

RON: You're in Elizabeth. Went from Jeffersonville to Elizabeth, Indiana. So what happened after Elizabeth, Indiana?

MAMA: Okay. While in Elizabeth—I will make this short—Momma needed—she wanted to go to the big market in New Albany.

So Daddy loaded up all the vegetables and stuff in a—I don't know what kind of vehicle it was. I drove her to New Albany.

RON: There's a big hill you come down from Elizabeth to New Albany too.

Was that on a Saturday?

MAMA: Yeah.

RON: Saturday market? Jinn and I go to a farmer's market on Saturday mornings in New Albany now.

MAMA: It's probably the same one. Isn't that amazing?

Of course, Momma, she knew how to do things. She could sell anything. And so I drove her to the market, and we made it just fine, but back then it was so different, you know. You didn't have to insure your car.

Daddy, he got homesick for Centertown. So we packed up and come back to Centertown, and that's where we ended up.

And, oh, the Blue Bus Café. When he moved back to Centertown, he was always wanting to entertain kids and people. So he thought up making a restaurant out of a bus, because he saw it parked in the woods down at Walton's Creek. He got that old bus—

RON: It was an old bus parked in the woods?

MAMA: Blue bus, yeah. It was a Greyhound. And he pulled it up there, remodeled it. It was pretty.

We had booths, jukebox, and he put a fireplace on one end. People could sit on each side. He used the bus seats, put on each side of the fireplace. And they had stools, and people could sit up there and order.

RON: Was this during World War II?

MAMA: Yeah. See, everything was rationed. Sugar, shoes, gas. Oh, Lord, I don't know what all, but Momma would get a few food stamps—I mean not food stamps. What were they called back then? War stamps or whatever, you know.

And my Grandmother Igleheart, she had some extra. So Momma would borrow hers, or Mammie would just give them to her to get sugar to make lemonade for that restaurant.

And everybody loved the way Momma cooked. She had grilled cheese, the best hamburgers you could ever taste, and lemonade, and whatever—I'm sure they had Coke. And people would flock to that restaurant. Of course, Daddy entertained them at night after he got done barbering.

RON: Did he entertain them with music and storytelling?

MAMA: Yeah.

RON: Did you ever sing with him?

MAMA: Not in the restaurant, no, but—let me see. That was—

RON: Blue Bus Café—about how many people lived in Centertown then?

MAMA: Oh, I don't know.

RON: 500 to 700?

MAMA: I don't have any idea.

RON: Not sure?

MAMA: It wasn't that much, but it was a booming town. We had three restaurants, pool room, churches everywhere, had a bank. I remember the—

RON: You had a pharmacy?

MAMA: Yeah, there was a funeral home, an old funeral home.

RON: Hardware.

MAMA: Yeah, the miner store, miners used to go to and trade at.

RON: Did you have a roller skating rink?

MAMA: We had a theater.

RON: A movie theater?

MAMA: Yeah.

RON: Wow.

MAMA: Roller skate. Daddy and I could really roller skate good. I loved it. Music to go skating.

RON: You taught me how to roller skate. I enjoyed it when I was a boy.

MAMA: Good. It was just a booming town.

RON: Did you all live at the Blue Bus Café?

MAMA: No, we lived in the back of it a while, and then we found—

RON: The house—

MAMA: The Olaton School.

RON: So Granddaddy attached that house to the Blue Bus Café?

MAMA: No, it was built back on another lot behind the Blue Bus Café.

RON: I remember that house. The barber shop was right in there, near there.

MAMA: The Blue Bus was hauled away when you was probably three years old. Jean Bennett come and hooked it up with a wrecker, but—and when Mom and Daddy—they moved back to Louisville when I got married and when you were born.

And he went back there and barbered and did some more grader work. He built the Watterson Expressway, and then started leveling off ground for the big mall there. And that's when the grader turned over on him.

RON: That was 1959.

MAMA: He was crushed.

RON: October of '59. I would have been nine the next month.

MAMA: And I got that call. It was terrible.

RON: I remember that call. It was.

MAMA: Oh, my gosh. Anyway, that was—

RON: Let's back up to Centertown and Blue Bus Café. You made the transition from the one room school house, Centertown School, grades 1 through 12. That was a big deal, wasn't it?

MAMA: Oh, it was, but see, I went on—still I went on to be in the first grade, because I didn't get to finish—I started at Walton's Creek so young, I was still in the first grade when we moved to Centertown. And that's when Jo Carolyn caught up with me see. We were in the same grade from then on.

RON: I didn't know that. So how did you like school? How did you do in school?

MAMA: I did good.

RON: I have often wondered about that.

MAMA: I did good. And my teacher, Ms. Elizabeth Calhoun, she was a Stenberg. She was a wonderful teacher.

And she would have these wonderful programs in the gymnasium. She got stories out of the old kids' storybooks, and she would put it all together for all of us kids to act in.

And I remember in the gymnasium when we had this one program, and the book—the leaves of the book would open up, and then the characters of that book would just walk out of—

RON: What kind of stories, like fairy tales?

MAMA: Yeah, yeah. We were all dressed up in whatever that story was about. And Jo and I were in that too. We were always in the programs. That was a big school.

RON: You liked your classes, you liked going to school, and did you do well in your classes?

MAMA: I sure did. I got an exempt from some of the big tests like science, I loved science. That was one of them I got exempt on. I was in the tenth grade then.

RON: Because you did so well?

MAMA: Uh-huh. Brian Taylor was my science teacher. It was a wonderful school. Now it's gone. What else do you want to talk about?

RON: Did you play any sports?

MAMA: Oh, heck yeah.

RON: You did?

MAMA: I was real good. I wanted to play baseball but back then they probably wouldn't have allowed a girl.

RON: Yeah.

MAMA: But I was really good at pitching. And when I got married, when you were young, I did, I did the fast pitch softball.

RON: During the war, World War II, that's when women's—

MAMA: That's when they got in to things, because all the men had to go to war.

RON: Yeah, they started doing jobs that men had done and started doing the sports that men had done.

MAMA: Oh, yeah, but see—anyway, I remember the guys that—in my group, we would have recess, and they would play marbles. And I loved to watch them play marbles because they were all different colors. I loved colors.

So I was standing by these two little Harper boys. One was struck on me. And every time he would win, he would give the marbles to me.

So I would go home with a pocket full of marbles every time they played marbles. Then I learned later that when he got out of school—that was a big deal, to play marbles—he was a champion marble player.

RON: It was a big deal.

MAMA: Yeah, but I don't know, we played jump the rope, hopscotch at school or recess.

RON: But you were athletic?

MAMA: Yeah, I was.

RON: Do you consider yourself to be something of a tomboy?

171

MAMA: Oh, yeah. I would climb a tree like a—skin a tree, like they used to say.

RON: Better than most of the boys or as good as any of the boys?

MAMA: This time I'm thinking about right now, is at Christmas. We—me and my friends—Jo was with us, and there was a boy that tagged along. He was always wanting to know what was going on with us girls.

Well, I wanted to go get a Christmas tree for Mom and Daddy. So we did, we went down the street and asked this couple if we could cross over the fence and get the Christmas tree we saw standing out in the field. And there were a couple of cows in there but that didn't faze us.

So I had a little hatchet and I cut down that tree and started carrying it home. Well, I carried it home. We might have taken turns—but not that little boy—and when I got it in the yard he tried to take it.

Well that's when I jumped him. He wasn't going to take that Christmas tree home. I fought for that tree and he went home crying.

RON: Well, Mama—

MAMA: Just things like that we did. When we moved to Centertown, we took Centertown over let me tell you.

RON: Oh, good. You took charge.

MAMA: Yeah.

RON: Mama, you have always—I have noticed that—and I think it runs in the Render side of the family—you have always been mischievous.

MAMA: Oh, Lord, yes. I got in trouble a few times being that way. I better not tell it.

RON: Well—

MAMA: I think I'll tell it.

I didn't like this girl at school, you know, different ones. I remember one, that she was kind of high uppity and—well, I will tell this on Jo before I tell one on me. She would come to school or go to church when we went and she would wear this pretty white jacket. And, of course, you know, we didn't care. We looked good. Momma made us look good. She sewed for us.

So this girl would strut around in that white coat, come to town. And we would be on the street, too. And so she said something to us. And there by Glenn's Grocery Store there was a ditch. So Jo got tired of her mouth and she shoved her over and got that pretty white coat all muddy. She pushed her in the ditch. We had had enough of that talking back to us.

I won't tell what I did one time.

RON: Oh, come on.

MAMA: Oh, it's silly.

RON: What did you do?

MAMA: Well, I didn't like this girl at school...

   (*end of tape two; beginning of tape three*)

MAMA: I'm going to back up and tell that dirty trick I played on this girl.

I mean, I love her now. She turned out to be a sweet girl. I was just aggravated at her then, some things she told, but anyway, I took dried up horse manure, put it in a box, shoe box, wrapped it up. And I saw her open it up, and I ran out of the room.

I guess you would call that a coward but she didn't know who sent it to her. That was it. I remember now, she didn't know who sent it to her.

RON: You sent her some dried up horse manure?

MAMA: Yeah.

RON: For her birthday?

MAMA: Either birthday or Christmas. That was awful.

RON: I have always loved your mischievous side, because I love you.

MAMA: Well, I tell you what, I have had some really—all of us have had some good times.

And Lord have mercy, we would turn loose, like I said, in Centertown, and we would go steal green apples at night from Mr. Morton's trees. They were the best apples.

And we'd just get a bunch together and get in the watermelon patch. We didn't do any damage. We just got us a watermelon to eat, but it was fun times back then.

All the kids in Centertown played. We thought up games to play, but there were always old-timey games of Anthony Over, Hopscotch and Kick the Can, and Hide and Seek was fun.

RON: Did you spend any time in graveyards or play at night any time, telling stories or anything like that?

MAMA: Oh, Lord, there were a lot of scary happenings in the graveyard. No.

I remember going home one night and walked past the Walton's Creek graveyard. There was some type of gas that comes up from the graves. And once in a while a light would flicker in the graveyard.

And later they explained it to me, that it was coming from the graves, the bodies, some way. I can't explain it to you, but anyway, that was a scary time.

RON: Mama, thank you for answering my questions, for telling these stories, sharing these stories, telling me things I never knew about your growing up years. And I look forward to this recording.

MAMA: Me too.

RON: I'm including these and lots of photos and other stories in your book—in the book I will be bringing out titled MAMA.

MAMA: I can't wait.

RON: All for you.

MAMA: I have had a good life. And a second good life started when I had you and got married and all my kids.

RON: I think the best way to build a bridge between your first 18 years and the next part of your story, the rest of your life, raising a family, having a family, kids, grandkids, greatgrandkids—

MAMA: Oh Lord, I just had my 25th great, and they're not even finished yet. I mean, there's two or three that haven't got married. I can't believe it.

RON: Well, let's finish the recording up with—I heard somebody say Brad is coming over. Paddy just got here. And Edie and Velvet are coming, and we will call Robin down in Miami and put her on speakerphone.

And let's close this thing out—build a bridge between your first 18 years and then your family-building years—with you, Mama, and all six of your kids singing Will the Circle Be Unbroken. Does that sound all right?

MAMA: Yes, yes.

RON: I love you, Mama.

MAMA: I love you. This has been fun. I'm tired.

RON: Well, go take a rest.

Song: Will the circle be unbroken, by and by, Lord, by and by. There's a better home awaiting in the sky, Lord, in the sky. Will the circle be unbroken, by and by, Lord, by and by. There's a better home awaiting in the sky, Lord, in the sky.

RON: That's the end of the recording. So just stop the recording there.

(*end of tape three; beginning of tape four*)

RON: This is Ron Whitehead. It's Wednesday, August 20, 2014, Beaver Dam, Kentucky, at Mama's kitchen table. And my mom is Greta Render Whitehead and

I'm working on a new book titled MAMA about Mama's life.

And this is the second interview session, and the final one, as well. We've made a lot of progress. The book will be filled with poems and stories and photos. And I would love for it to come out this fall but it will certainly come out no later than spring.

So today will be a short interview, and then I will head back the old way to Louisville and get back to work on the book. And I'm working on a second book, as well, called Kentucky Basketball, Poetry in Motion.

The first interviews took us from Mama's birth up until she was ready to start a family.

Back up just a little bit here and discuss—we're going to discuss the beginnings of her family life and then we will spend a little time there, not too much, whatever Mama wants to, and then we'll jump ahead to the end of Daddy's life.

That will be the epilogue of the book and Mama's life in the past five years. She can touch on that briefly, what she has been up to and what she is up to now. Okay. Hi, Mama.

MAMA: Hi. Hi, Ron.

RON: Mama, when did you and Daddy first meet? Do you remember—

MAMA: Oh, man.

RON: --when and where? I have always wondered about that. Was it at the Blue Bus Café or just around Centertown?

MAMA: No, just around Centertown.

RON: It's a small town.

MAMA: One of the other restaurants, early restaurants, other than Blue Bus.

RON: What was the name of the other restaurant?

MAMA: Bishop's was one.

RON: Bishop's, the same people that owned the drug store?

MAMA: My Aunt Rena managed one of them.

No, it wasn't the same people.

Anyway, back then, I mean, kids, they didn't grow up as fast as they do now. I mean, good Lord, I probably carried a doll and played with dolls when I was 13, 14 years old.

But we were playing outside the restaurant. Kids played everywhere in Centertown. And your dad told me this: he was sitting in the car with this Chancellor guy, and the guy said look at that little girl there, she is going to be something else. And your dad told him, he said I'm going to marry her.

And so probably a year later, you know, he got to talk to me with—out in front of the restaurant with a bunch of other guys, and he got to talk to me.

And anyway, he made plans to take me to a movie with another couple. So the couple and—your dad and the other couple come up to our house. And I went out to get in the car, and the other girl was—she was going to sit up front with your dad.

Well, I don't know what I did but I got in that front seat because I was going to sit by your dad and go to the movie. She wasn't going—she was going to crowd in.

Anyway, that was probably the first so-called date with another couple, went to see a movie.

RON: Did Daddy have a reputation when you met him, word on the street about Daddy or anything, or what did you think of him?

MAMA: You would call him a—probably a lady's man now. He was a—he could be a smart aleck. He was flirty.

Your dad was a cocky guy. He and his brothers, they were—I would call them bad. They were something else.

RON: Nobody messed with them?

MAMA: No, nobody messed with them, but anyway, that was the start of our relationship.

And we might have gone to another movie or two. I went to a ball game with him once, I remember, in Fordsville. And I was real nervous about going to that ball game with him.

I mean, he was—he seemed so much smarter than me, which he was. And I was afraid, you know, he would probably ask me something that I didn't feel like commenting on, but anyway, it was the beginning of our relationship.

RON: Well, how old were you then, 16, 17, 15?

MAMA: No, I was 17.

RON: Seventeen?

MAMA: Yeah. Let's see, it was probably—when we got married I had just turned 18. I turned 18 in May. We got married in April.

RON: So did you-all get your first home together after you got married?

MAMA: No. Your dad worked at the mines. He started working at the mines at an early age, probably—he was 17, I think. And it was—when we got married—we got married with another couple that was real close to us, Margie and Ralph.

Margie Romans was kind of related to your dad, and Ralph Boyd. They were close friends with us.

So he and Ralph planned this, the get-together wedding. So we went to Preacher Boyd's house in Centertown and stood up with Margie and Ralph, and they went with us to a preacher's house over in Utica, close to Utica, and they stood up with us there.

RON: Utica in Daviess County.

MAMA: Well, yeah.

RON: Near McLean County.

MAMA: It wasn't too far out of Hartford. We honeymooned together. We went to Owensboro, and on Highway 60 there was a little row of cute little cabins.

And so we—your daddy and Ralph went and picked one out. And the rooms were connected, you know. There was a divider door, but we honeymooned in the same little cabin.

But that was really neat, to stay in a little cabin like that. I thought it was really something special.

And so when your dad, he had to go back to work Monday morning after that. He was so devoted to his job. That's all the honeymoon we had, was just over the weekend.

And we made our home—our first home—with his sister and her husband out of Centertown.

RON: Which sister?

MAMA: It was Lois and Rethel, yeah. And they had a big house. And we had a bedroom, of course, of our own. I helped her in the kitchen. She was so sweet. They were sweet and kind to us and enjoyed us being there.

And then a little apartment—it was a house, but the house was divided. And we got two rooms on the left side. Then another one of our friends, a couple, they got the other side.

And what was funny, I knew how to cook back then, because I have always helped my mom and my brother and sisters. So I would fix a nice—a good meal for your dad when he would come in from work.

Here comes the couple next door knocking on the door. So I had—you know, you have to invite them in for supper. They smelled my food cooking. And she was a little on the awry side, I won't say who it was, but we had friends for supper a lot of nights.

RON: Really?

MAMA: Then after that we—well, okay. You come along next. We were still in that little apartment house and I was getting everything ready for Thanksgiving. November, of course, and I was going to fix a big meal.

I had my hot rolls planned out, turkey and all the side dishes, and I was going to have my mom and dad and my brothers and sisters.

Well, early that morning, Thanksgiving—really early Thanksgiving morning—I started having labor pains. And your dad was going to go hunting with his brothers.

Well, okay. I have to say, you knocked all that in the head. You wanted to be born on Thanksgiving Day.

And I went to the hospital—we went to the hospital with my mom and dad taking us or riding with us. And they came in my room and they had a big old turkey leg, trying to get me to eat Thanksgiving meal. Of course, I couldn't do it.

But that night late when you were born, it come the biggest snowfall. It was a record breaker, I'm sure. And my mom and dad—well, your dad went with them back to Centertown. They had a very hard time getting home.

I remember your—or my—dad saying that here comes a car at them, towards them. All of a sudden, it just disappeared.

RON: Down Hoover Hill.

MAMA: They didn't know where in the world it went to. And that was—call that the hand of God seeing after them, trying to get them home.

And it snowed and snowed. And, of course, back then you had to stay at least six days.

RON: When you had a baby.

MAMA: But at the hospital your dad was so happy to have a little boy. He called his mom and dad. They had that old wall telephone, and his mom picked up the receiver, and your dad shouted I've got a little boy. I named you before I left the hospital.

RON: And so when you went home from the hospital, where was home?

MAMA: That little apartment house. That little apartment, two rooms.

RON: How much longer did you live there?

MAMA: Oh, it wasn't too much longer after that. Your dad wanted a place for us to have by ourselves.

So we rented a little block house down by—well, it was across from the post office, real cute little concrete block house.

RON: Near the jailhouse?

MAMA: Yeah, yeah, so-called jailhouse.

RON: Yeah, I remember, post office, jailhouse.

MAMA: And, of course, I knew how to fix things up. I knew how to make a house a home. I loved doing it. I would make my own curtains. And if I couldn't find the material I would tear up an old sheet and sew up some pretty little curtains with some ruffles on them.

I remember one time I was sewing on the sewing machine, the treadle sewing machine. And I was making you a cute little pair of shorts for summer. And the needle got loose and went right straight through my finger by my fingernail.

So I unscrewed that part of the sewing machine, and I got you by the hand, and we walked up to my mom and dad's house. And she took me to the emergency room—or to the doctor's office. We didn't have—the hospital wasn't open then, that year. And he pulled it out and put some kind of antiseptic on it.

And I think I was pregnant with Brad. Yeah, I believe I was when that happened, but nothing bothered me. I mean, I just walked up to mom and dad's house down the street with a needle sticking through my hand.

RON: So in those early years when I was born and Brad came along, Mamaw and Granddaddy, did they leave to go back to Louisville when you were pregnant with me?

MAMA: Oh, no, no.

RON: Because you said you walked up to their house. So I was a little boy, so—

MAMA: They were still there. Daddy was still barbering and doing grading work around town, or for the county. And—no, when—they moved to Louisville when Brad was born, a little boy.

RON: Okay.

MAMA: So we moved to their house.

RON: Because I have the vaguest memories, just close, near the surface there of them still being down there.

MAMA: Well—

RON: So I guess—

MAMA: —they would come home a lot.

RON: When I was two, that's probably it, them coming back down.

MAMA: You were two—now, Brad was—he was—he might have been a year old. I don't know, but we moved to their house. And we thought we were really up town, because it was a nice little house my dad built, and Momma had it decorated real pretty.

RON: We lived there for two years before we moved to the farm? That was a nice house.

MAMA: Well, yeah. Paddy was born when we lived in that house. She was born in the Daviess County Hospital.

RON: She is five years younger than me, yeah.

MAMA: Yeah. And the Blue Bus Café was still there. And let's see. Brigance—the Brigance guy, he ran it, and his wife.

She wanted to baby-sit you. Well, they didn't have any children and so I let you go down there a lot. And they were so crazy about you. They would set you up on the—up on that little—

RON: At the Blue Bus Café?

MAMA: Yeah.

RON: I'll be. That's actually in my blood, in my memory?

MAMA: Yeah. And I have got a picture of Gene Bennett's little wrecker hauling the Blue Bus Café away. And you were on a tricycle outside it as they were moving it.

RON: Well, I would like to see that. I would like to include that in the book.

MAMA: Okay, if I can find it. It might be in your album.

RON: I don't think so. Do you have any photos of me in the Blue Bus Café?

MAMA: No. I wish I did.

RON: Doggone it.

MAMA: I wish I did. That was the end of—what do you want to call it?

RON: End of an era.

MAMA: Yeah, because that was back during the Korean War.

RON: It was there for several years, then?

MAMA: They were the last ones to operate the Blue Bus Café—because they wanted to take that over when mom and dad moved to Louisville.

Yeah, we moved out to the farm when Paddy was a little girl, little—well, I guess she was.

RON: She was just born.

MAMA: I think she was six, seven months old.

RON: Yeah, because it was wintertime. I remember it being cold.

MAMA: She was born in August. And we would go out there in March and paint. We had an old coal stove, and your dad would fire that thing up. He worked second shift.

And we would stay there, and you all would play around the little room that I was painting in. I would paint the walls while he would go work his shift. And I would take snacks. And he would come back and paint a little bit and then we would go back to Centertown.

And then we finally got it all fixed and moved out there and that was the beginning of your-all's life on the farm. Cattle, pigs, and one milk cow. I remember helping your dad milk. We had to do a lot of things like that when you got bigger because your dad worked late at the mines. And if he would come home at dark we would have the work done for him.

RON: Yeah.

MAMA: He worked hard at the mines. Very hard.

RON: He was there for 43 years, wasn't he?

MAMA: It was close to that.

RON: Well, we had animals even when we were in town. And we were always visiting relatives on farms and friends on farms and everybody had animals.

MAMA: Well, we always had a dog.

RON: I always loved animals.

MAMA: We had chickens. I remember one time when we lived in town, I had ordered some chickens—little chickens.

RON: I remember those little chicks.

MAMA: We were getting ready to go to the farm so I wanted some chickens.

So the post office let me know that my chickens were there. We went down there, and they were peep peeping, and I—

RON: They came in the mail?

MAMA: Yeah. I had a box of them. There were 25.

RON: I swear.

MAMA: And there were several boxes for people that ordered the chickens. It was so cute.

I had to fix up a little pen for them in the kitchen. And we had to keep them warm because they were little babies.

And we would put a light bulb—fixed a light bulb for them to hang over the box to keep them warm.

RON: I remember that.

MAMA: And fed them, fixed them a little water thing out of a fruit jar and a saucer. And when the saucer got empty the water would ease out and they could get something to drink. You turn the jar upside down, let the water seep out gradually.

RON: Jinn and I went to the state fair last year. And I had been telling Jinn that Daddy was the best shot anywhere and the story about him—his dad giving him one shell during the Depression and what a good shot you are, and what a great shot I am, and I think she really didn't believe me.

Then we went to the fair, to one of the booths. I think it's Kentucky Department of Agriculture, and they got targets and you shoot. And I hit every one of them, didn't miss a one. And the woman said you're the best that's been here all day.

That really impressed Jinn. I said I have been an expert marksman since I was two years old. She said you have not. I said I got my first gun when I was two.

There's a photo of me with a BB gun. I know I was little, and Daddy was real big on us being good marksmen, because he was.

Do you remember when—he probably let me shoot a .22 or something when I was two.

MAMA: Probably, but he got you a .410. I got a picture of you.

RON: I had a .410 for years. That was my gun for a long time. I loved a .410. Over and under, .22 above, .410 under.

MAMA: I still have it.

RON: You still have it?

MAMA: Yeah. It's yours.

RON: I swear.

MAMA: But I'm guarding my house with it now.

RON: That's the one—

MAMA: Yeah.

RON: --that you shot a hole in the floor with?

MAMA: Yeah. It's a single shot.

RON: All right. Well, okay.

MAMA: Your dad was a good shot. He would have us throw up tin cans and bottles.

RON: I remember. He could shoot them with a .22, bottles, cans, anything.

MAMA: Pistol. He loved the pistol.

RON: He would draw the pistol—you throw something up and he would draw and shoot it in the air.

Yeah, he was as good as Annie Oakley. I wrote a story I just posted about you shooting and us kids calling you Annie Oakley.

MAMA: I would like to shoot the old blackbirds here but I live in Beaver Dam city limits, darn it.

I told the law man one time, I said I'm going to start shooting blackbirds. He said well, I think you better walk a few feet over in the field.

On the Fourth of July when all the fireworks are going on around here I shoot the .410. I do.

RON: That's funny. Well, and I know you went hunting some too because I already—

MAMA: I like to go squirrel hunting. I went with your dad.

RON: I always liked eating squirrel gravy and biscuits and squirrel.

MAMA: Oh, yes.

RON: We had that for breakfast many times.

Well, is there anything that stands out for you in the early years of you being a mother? I mean, how did you feel about being a mother?

MAMA: I loved being pregnant. I mean, I did—I just got up every morning like a normal morning and I waited on you all, cooked breakfast, got your dad off to work.

I mean, it was a joy to be pregnant and have that little baby come into this world. And I didn't—I never had any trouble, so—

RON: Well, did—

MAMA: You kids worked hard on the farm, if you want to talk about that. You brought in hay. We worked in the tobacco. We didn't have that much. We had five tenths, half acre.

RON: Half acre is more—when you're working, it's a lot more than you think.

MAMA: Seemed like two or three, especially when it rains and rains and rains, and you got to pick it out.

RON: Oh, I know, and hoeing it. And those rows look so long, especially when you're a little kid. And suckering it. I hated suckering it and topping.

MAMA: I remember one time—my brothers and sisters were always at our house. Of course, we loved having them. And my brothers come down one summer to stay a while, and you all went to help Wayland Render chop out his tobacco.

RON: Oh, yeah. He was hard to work for.

MAMA: Well, Timmy came back to the house. And your dad said what are you doing back here, you're supposed to be working in the tobacco. He said it's tiresome. He said oh, it's tiresome.

RON: I remember Brad and Timmy and me going in that patch, and he wouldn't just send us into the patch. He stood at the end of the row like an old overseer, like a slave master. And he would bitch and gripe about stuff all the time.

MAMA: That helped you get down to the other end, I guess.

RON: Yeah, yeah. And Timmy—I don't know if he made it to the end of the first row or not. And Wayland was chewing on him. He said what are you doing, boy, standing there. And Timmy finally just walked out of the patch and walked home.

MAMA: That's when he came back to the house.

RON: That was funny.

MAMA: But Timmy now, he is just like his daddy. He is like our daddy. He has got the beautiful playgrounds for all the kids to play on when we have reunions.

RON: It's amazing. What he has built there is better than most state parks.

MAMA: I call it the Dick Render playground. It's something else.

RON: Granddaddy built that amusement—the carnival amusement park.

MAMA: He built a Ferris wheel, yeah. Kids loved it, right beside his barber shop.

But anyway, back to Wayland, you all loved Wayland.

RON: Yeah, I thought the world of Wayland.

MAMA: He become a Representative for our area. And you all loved going places with him. He was at our house all the time talking to you all and having supper.

RON: Yeah, almost every day at meal time he would knock on the door.

MAMA: Because his family was hardly ever around.

RON: Yeah. Lived down there on the hill, Cedar Hill is what he called it.

MAMA: I think so. What it looked like, anyway.

RON: We used to go down there with Daddy and listen to UK basketball games at night, and we'd go down and listen to Cassius Clay fights on the radio.

MAMA: He would get tickets, see.

RON: We had the best seats in the house.

MAMA: You all got to go with him all the time.

RON: Yeah. I thought the world of him.

Well, all right. There's just so many things we could talk about.

MAMA: I know it.

RON: Too many directions to go in.

MAMA: Well, we could—you know, when your dad started getting sick, having trouble with his heart—

RON: He had the heart attack six months after he retired from the coal mines. And they thought he was going to die that night.

MAMA: So from then on I was so concerned and worried about him, I would—he would stop breathing in the night. And I stayed awake a lot of nights just hoping that he would, you know—

RON: Be okay.

MAMA: —wasn't going—I was just afraid he wasn't going to make it some nights, it was so bad.

RON: I remember at the hospital, the doctor saying he couldn't believe that he had lived through the heart attack. He lost half his heart. It would have killed most NFL football players, he said.

And he said that he might give him two or three days, the doctor said, I remember. And then after three days he said well, he might make it three months. And then he kept extending it, and Daddy lived what, 18 years, I think?

MAMA: A good while, yeah.

RON: It was a bunch of years.

MAMA: He went back to doing things on the farm. Of course, he loved the farm. That's what kept him going, too, loving the farm.

RON: But he finally just got wore down so much he couldn't do it.

MAMA: Yeah, we finally had to sell out.

RON: Yeah. Well—

MAMA: It was a good life for all of you.

RON: Yeah, it was.

How are you doing here in Beaver Dam now, Mama? Five years after Daddy died, how are you doing? You're 82 years old now.

MAMA: I'm doing good. I mean, I know I have to. I'm not like some women that just, you know, gets up and cries every day. That's not going—that's not good.

RON: You got the best attitude anybody could have.

MAMA: So your daddy and I loved going out and being with our friends for breakfast. And we—some nights we'd go down to the restaurant and have our supper, and he loved doing that. He loved being retired.

So we would go out about every morning for breakfast. And it was a round table at The Wagon Wheel Restaurant. And all of our friends would congregate there. We had some really good discussions and laughs.

So when he died, I would get up every morning, and I would continue going. And some people would look at me, and I know what they were thinking. What is she doing, you know, coming out here by herself.

Well, I had friends, and I wanted to stay friends with them. And they would come by and have breakfast with me.

RON: It's good that you stayed active, too.

MAMA: I'm the type to—I don't take things—death like some people, because death is—

RON: Part of life.

MAMA: Well, yeah. And you know you're going to be with that person again if you're a Christian.

So I grieve a different way.

RON: And we have been through so many deaths, too.

MAMA: Yeah. And when I hear a song or watch a love story, a movie, it makes me sad and I cry, but—

RON: I'm the same way.

MAMA: —you got to go on. I got kids, grandkids and great—25 great now. They're not even—some—three or four of them are not even married yet.

RON: I saw somewhere in your notes, Mama, that you told Daddy somewhere along the line that once the kids were all grown, you were going to become a writer. I read that. You wrote it down. And now you are.

MAMA: I love to write.

RON: You're writing this book as much as I am.

MAMA: But one reason why writing is good for you, is the things that I think of and I can't tell another person right then, because they're not there, so I write about that. And it keeps my hands—you know, people get old. Their fingers don't work. Keeps my hands—

RON: Nimble.

MAMA: Yeah.

And I love to keep a document of the weather. Your dad loved that. We could always go back two or three years and see what the weather was that certain day.

And we have had—so far we have had ten August fogs. And the old-timers always said, every fog in August means a snow in the winter.

RON: Oh, is that right? I didn't know that.

MAMA: All of them have been right except—I think it was yesterday, it was dense. You couldn't hardly see the—I couldn't see my neighborhood.

So we have had—today we've had 11 fogs in August. That's a lot.

RON: That's 11 more days. That's interesting.

Well, last winter seemed the longest winter ever. This is the mildest summer I remember ever. So 11 fogs in August—so we're going to have a bunch of snow this winter.

MAMA: Yeah, no doubt.

RON: Interesting.

Mama, let me ask you this, and we will conclude the interview part of this new book and recording project.

What plans do you have at 82? In so many ways you have lived such a rich life, but in so many ways, every day is a new beginning.

Do you have any specific plans for the future?

MAMA: No plans to marry, I tell you that much.

RON: Okay. Well, that's a plan.

MAMA: I love being here. Of course, I would love to have your dad, but I love getting up, doing my own thing, running through the house naked if I like to, and turn the music up loud, and just get up every morning.

I love to go to breakfast still. I got two guys I eat breakfast with. One has lost his wife, and the other one is—she is in the rest home with Alzheimer's.

So I enjoy being with them. One is a real cut-up, and the other one is serious but very intelligent. They're both real smart guys.

But I would love to have a guy to, you know, call me and say let's go eat out and go to a movie or something, but I don't have that.

RON: Yeah.

MAMA: They're both up in their 80s, and—

RON: We can see that happening in the future, then.

MAMA: Well, I have had several guys that asked me if I was going to marry again. And I told them right off, I just couldn't afford to marry again, anyway.

It's not right for a woman. A woman can—you know, when she marries again she loses her insurance and, you know.

RON: Oh, yeah, yeah.

MAMA: And her—no telling what, but no.

RON: Well, Mama—

MAMA: Marrying again is not for me.

RON: Do you have a final word for anybody out there—family, friends, strangers, anybody out there—any word—final word of wisdom to pass on to the present and future generations?

MAMA: Well, I always loved this song. My mom did too.

Song: One day at a time, sweet Jesus. One day at a time...

RON: That's the best way to handle it.

MAMA: I get up every morning, glad to put my foot out on the floor, my feet.

RON: There you go. Be thankful for that day.

MAMA: Oh, yeah.

RON: Yeah. That's the way I live, too.

MAMA: Even if it's cloudy. Cloudy day, rainy day.

Last night I looked in the north, and there was the most beautiful lightning show that I have never seen. It was a storm. The weatherman said it was in Indiana. And I watched that for 20 minutes.

RON: Nice.

MAMA: I love a thunderstorm.

RON: Me too. Okay, Mama, thank you. I'm real excited about this book and this recording.

MAMA: Me too. I have had a wonderful life, beautiful family, talented. And they all love and respect me. And I'm looking forward to more greatgrandkids and marriages.

RON: Good. Thanks, Mama. And as your oldest child—thank you for doing this project with me. I just want to tell you how much I love you.

MAMA: I love you too. It's been a joy, Ron.

RON: It has. Thank you!!

(end of tape four)

Acknowledgements

Special thanks to the editors of the following publications in which the listed poems previously appeared, some in slightly different form.

TriQuarterly (and multiple other publications): "Mama"

The New Southerner: "stevie fell out"

The New Southerner: "arriving"

Levure Littéraire (and multiple other publications): "the dance"

About the Authors

Greta Render Whitehead *was born in 1932, in Matanzas, Kentucky, to Raymond and Louverine Render. She is the oldest of thirteen children. In 1950 she married Edwin Whitehead. They have six children, sixteen grandchildren, and twenty seven great grandchildren. This is her first book. Greta lives in Beaver Dam, Kentucky.*

Poet, writer, editor, publisher, scholar, activist **Ron Whitehead** *is the author of 30 books and 40 cds. He has performed thousands of shows, with musicians and bands, round the world. He has produced over 3,000 poetry & music events, festivals, and non-stop 24 & 48 & 72 & 90 hour Insomniacathons throughout Europe and the USA.*

He has published over 2,000 titles including works by Jack Kerouac, Allen Ginsberg, William S. Burroughs, Neal Cassady, Lawrence Ferlinghetti, Gregory Corso, Herbert Huncke, David Amram, Diane di Prima, Amiri Baraka, Ed Sanders, Anne Waldman, Hunter S. Thompson, Andy Warhol, Yoko Ono, Jim Carroll, Bono, Robert Hunter, Lee Ranaldo, Frank Messina, Birgitta Jonsdottir, Douglas Brinkley, E. Ethelbert Miller, Michael Dean Odin Pollock, Jan Kerouac, John Updike, Rita Dove, Eithne

Strong, Theo Dorgan, President Jimmy Carter, Seamus Heaney, Thomas Merton, Robert Lax, Edvard Munch, Knut Hamsun, Jean Genet, James Laughlin, Brother Patrick Hart, Wendell Berry, His Holiness The Dalai Lama and many others. He wrote the poem Never Give Up with The Dalai Lama.

He recently returned from a Finland and Estonia Tour where he was the featured poet at four international arts festivals. When not traveling the world he home bases at his hermitage on Cherokee Road in The Highlands of Louisville, Kentucky.

When you're a rural Kentucky boy
with an account at the general store
because your daddy has steady work
at the mines, why, it requires more
than a little nerve to leave the tobacco fields,
run past 9-to-5, take the hurdles and
the long jump, land, and be a poet.

When you're a rural Kentucky boy
wearing flowered shirts and purple scarves,
with a face tattoo you got in Estonia
and both ears pierced, why, you might be
inviting stares at the diner when you visit Mama
but the rush of feeling at the Fair among
the hay, the honey, the pigs, the tractors...

oh, it takes you by surprise each time.

Afterword

> the strongest and best men
> aren't nearly as strong
> or as good as one good
> strong Mother

In the summer of 2014 I was the featured poet at four international festivals in Finland and Estonia. On a nine hour train ride from Lapland to southern Finland I recalled reading a book about Finland when I was a boy growing up on a Kentucky farm. And for the first time visiting Finland I was surprised by the many similarities between Kentucky and Finland: trees and lakes and friendly faces everywhere. I like Finland, the people and the place.

While reminiscing about my childhood I was suddenly struck with the realization that I knew nearly nothing about Mama's growing up years. I had been restless and hungry to venture into new directions with my creative work so I instantly decided to write a book about Mama's early life. While receiving the vision for the creative project it occurred to me to invite Mama to write the book with me and that it would include poems and stories by both of us plus photos plus I'd do interviews with her. When I got back to Kentucky

I called Mama and shared my ideas for the project with her. She was so excited. She said Yes!

Later, as I was going through stacks of handwritten journals and notes and letters and photographs I found a torn piece of paper with a message from Mama to Daddy, "Ed, when the kids are grown I'm going to become a writer." And now, at age 83, Mama is a published author!

MAMA: a poet's heart in a kentucky girl is a treasure beyond measure. Thank you Mama!

I Love You!

Ronnie Paige
September 2015

www.ingramcontent.com/pod-product-compliance
Lightning Source LLC
Chambersburg PA
CBHW060513100426
42743CB00009B/1299